Classic to Contemporary
String Quilts

Techniques, Inspiration, and 16 Projects for Strip Quilting

Mary M. Hogan

Landauer Publishing

Classic to Contemporary String Quilts

by Mary M. Hogan

Landauer Publishing (*www.landauerpub.com*) is an imprint of
Fox Chapel Publishing Company, Inc.

Copyright © 2019 by Mary M. Hogan and
Fox Chapel Publishing Company, Inc., 903 Square Street, Mount Joy, PA 17552.

Project Team:
Vice President-Content: Christopher Reggio
Editors: Laurel Albright/Sue Voegtlin
Copy Editor: Jeremy Hauck
Designer: Laurel Albright
Photographer: Sue Voegtlin

ISBN: 978-1-947163-04-1

The Cataloging-in-Publication Data is on file with the Library of Congress.

We are always looking for talented authors.
To submit an idea, please send a brief inquiry to
acquisitions@foxchapelpublishing.com.

Printed in Singapore

21 20 19   2 4 6 8 10 9 7 5 3 1

What else can I do with strings?

Contents

48 String Quilt Projects

Night Flight Quilt 50

Carpenter Star Quilt 56

Circling Geese Quilt 62

String Churn Dash Quilt 68

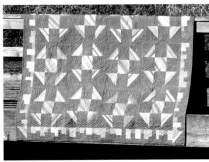

Shoo Fly Quilt 74

Rainbow Sherbet Quilt 80

Starry, Starry Night Quilt 86

Card Trick
Table Topper 92

Dresden Plate Wall Hanging 98

Dresden Plate Table Runner 104

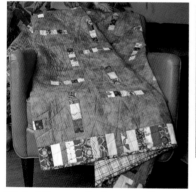

This Way and That Quilt 108

Confetti Columns Quilt 114

Four Seasons
of Trees Wall
Hangings 120

126 Terms and Definitions

127 About the Author/Resources

Strings Make Quilts Unique

After completing work on my first book, *String Quilt Style*, I asked myself, "What else can I do with strings?" Instead of placing a solid piece of fabric in a position for a classic quilt block, such as the String Churn Dash, page 68, I covered that block section with strings. I absolutely loved how it looked. The strings added so much interest, and there was so much more to look at in each block section. Taking a traditional block and interpreting it with strings, transformed it, giving it a fresh, contemporary look.

I relaxed my rules of perfection. Strings are allowed to be crooked, they can include the selvage, or a contrasting skinny strip. A few of the projects in the book are contemporary and have no equivalent, traditional design: Confetti Columns, page 114; This Way and That, page 108; and Four Seasons of Trees, page 120. They were made in response to that same question, "What else can I do with strings?" My hope is that you will be inspired by what you see here, and you'll give strings a try. But most of all, have fun quilting!

Tools and Foundations

Stitching string blocks is similar to stitching any pieced block, except the strings are sewn to a foundation of paper or background fabric. No specialty tools are required and only basic sewing supplies are needed.

ESSENTIAL TOOLS

+ Rotary cutter and cutting mat
+ Rulers
+ Straight pins
+ Flathead pins
+ Sewing machine
+ Thread
+ Scissors

SOME OF MY FAVORITE TOOLS

+ 6" x 24" (15.24 x 60.96cm) and 3" x 18" (7.62 x 45.72cm) rulers

+ 18" x 24" (45.72 x 60.96cm) cutting mat for cutting strings

+ Rotating cutting mat for trimming blocks

+ Bent tweezers to remove bits of foundation

FOUNDATIONS AND BACKGROUNDS

Foundations and background fabrics are used in these projects as a guide for placement of strings. Paper foundations serve as patterns and keep blocks flat as strings are added. I look for foundations that provide support as string blocks are made, that are easy to remove, and are low cost. Backgrounds provide the basis for many projects. As one example, a background square is the guide for adding strings to cover one side to make half-square triangles. The Night Flight Quilt, page 50, uses two blocks made this way to create Flying Geese Blocks.

Removable foundations include newsprint, copy paper, drawing paper, parchment paper, and coffee filters. Fabric strings are sewn to the paper foundations and trimmed. The paper is removed before sewing blocks together. These products can be found at office supply stores, restaurant suppliers and grocery stores.

Start Stringing! The Basics

While you can use precut strips, string quilts typically utilize fabric you already have. String piecing is easy and for more experienced quilters, provides a welcome break from detailed piecing. Strings are sewn to a foundation or background fabric, and then trimmed. Most projects using traditional blocks are done at a larger scale to ease construction. Precise sewing is not as crucial as when stitching pieced block sections. Blocks often include some surprise elements, such as a really crooked string, a selvage string, or a contrasting skinny strip. Rules of perfection are relaxed. Lines within a block section are encouraged to be a little wonky. For example, triangles may be somewhat crooked. Make it your way. *As long as each block section is trimmed to the correct size, everything will fit.*

PREPARING AND CUTTING STRINGS

Cutting fabric strings is easy. Any fabric left over from another project or fabric from your stash can be cut into varying widths and set aside for a string quilt. Toss strings, regardless of width, in a bin or bags. Some projects do require specific sized strings, so if you have a project in mind, check the instructions before cutting your strings.

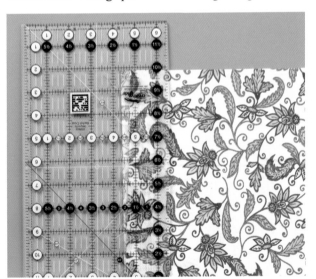

1. Press the fabrics before cutting. There is no need to square up uneven edges since pieces like this can used for Crooked Strings, page 34, or Disappearing Strings, page 36). Using a rotary cutter and ruler, cut a first string.

2. Continue cutting strings in a variety of widths.

3. A variety of lengths are needed so don't discard shorter strings. Leftover fabric scraps can be used to cut crooked strings, cover a corner, or pieced to make longer strings.

CUTTING SELVAGES

Selvages can add a unique touch to a string quilt. If you plan to incorporate selvages into your quilt, save some as you cut fabrics. Line up a ruler on the selvage edge and cut a 1½"-wide (3.81cm) strip. This will give you the selvage, as well as some of the color and pattern of the fabric.

STRING WIDTHS

In general, strings for these projects range from 1" (2.54cm) to 2½" (6.35cm), but review the instructions before cutting strings for a specific project. The width of strings should be proportional to the area that needs to be covered. For example, the smaller Flying Geese in Circling Geese, page 62, uses much smaller strings than the Flying Geese in Night Flight. Include some crooked or angled strings; they will make your blocks more interesting.

Before you cut!

Decide your width of string preferences and how many strings you need.

Keep colors separate— plastic zipper bags work well.

Fabric requirements are given but scraps from your stash can be used for strings, too. Even short pieces can be used for smaller blocks, for finishing corners, or for disappearing strings. Try making a longer string using several short pieces. Use up some smaller bits of fabric and add interest to your string piecing.

CHOOSING FOUNDATIONS OR BACKGROUND FABRIC BLOCKS

String piecing is taking a variety of strips or scrap strips and sewing them onto a paper foundation or background fabric, to make a quilt block. The paper is removed from the back of a block, and background fabric becomes a part of the block design.

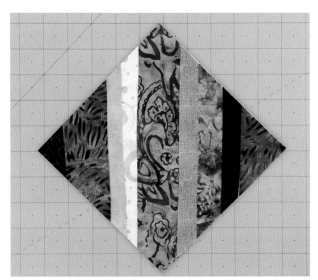
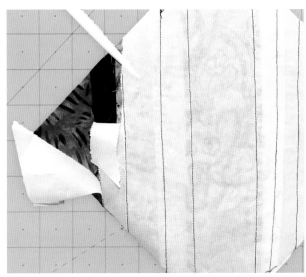

Paper foundations are used when blocks are entirely covered with strings. The paper foundation becomes the guide for trimming the blocks. After trimming, the paper foundation is removed from the back of the block.

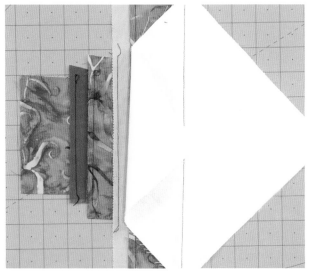

Background fabric becomes a part of the block design. The first string is sewn to the fabric and as strings are added, the background fabric is folded out of the way so that additional strings are only sewn to a previous string. When the block is finished, the fabric under the strings is trimmed off, leaving strings and background fabric as part of the block.

MARKING PAPER FOUNDATION AND BACKGROUND FABRIC BLOCKS

Strings are sewn to blocks starting in the middle, and additional strings are sewn to the left and right of the center string. Some patterns tell you to center a seam line in the block, splitting the block exactly down the middle, either diagonally or vertically. Other patterns tell you to center a string randomly, at about the diagonal center or vertical center.

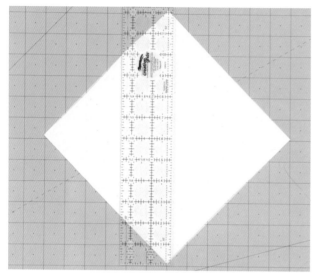

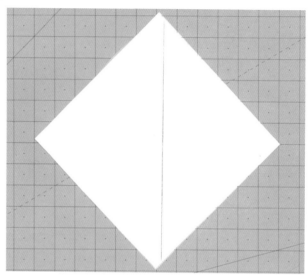

1. Select the correct size foundation or background fabric needed for a block. Place a ruler ¼" (0.64cm) to the right of the diagonal center and draw a line. If you are marking a square, draw the line ¼" (0.64cm) to the right of the vertical center.

2. Use this mark to align the raw edge of your first string. Sewing ¼" (0.64cm) away from the drawn line will center the seam on your block.

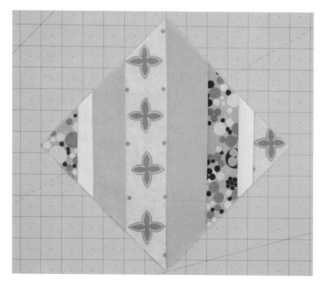

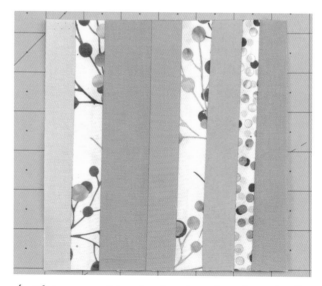

3. The seam is centered in the block.

4. The green string is about centered vertically. No line is needed for this technique.

FOUNDATION PAPER STRING BLOCKS

Marking, sewing, and trimming string blocks is pretty simple and the following basics apply to the projects in the book. Only three projects (Shoo Fly, page 74; Rainbow Sherbet, page 80; and Carpenter Star, page 56) require foundation paper block sections. Use a slightly smaller stitch length when sewing on paper foundations. The stitches perforate the paper, making it easier to remove when the block is finished.

Diagonal Square Block

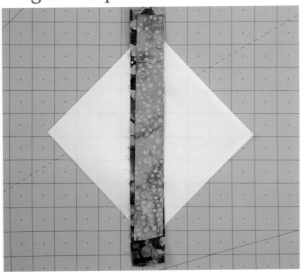

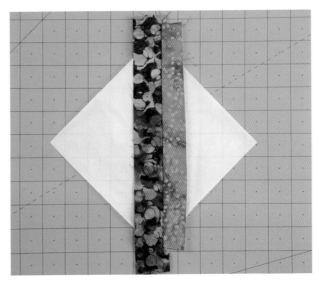

1. Select the paper foundation size needed for the block. Place a string right side up on about the diagonal center. Place another string right side down on the first string, matching the right raw edges.

2. Sew the strings with a ¼" (0.64cm) seam. Open the string and press.

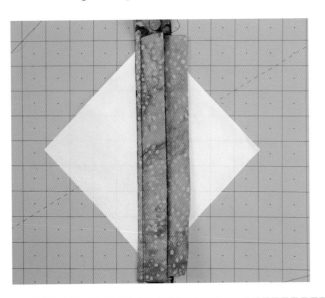

3. Select another string, place it right sides together, matching the left raw edges. Sew with a ¼" (0.64cm) seam. Open the string and press.

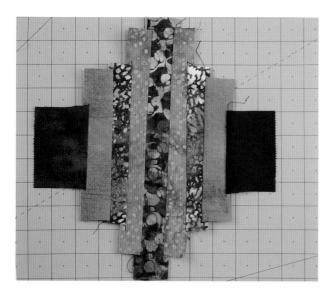

4. Continue adding the strings to the left and right of the center string until the paper is completely covered. Open and press each string before adding a new one.

5. Turn the block over and trim, using the foundation as the trimming guide.

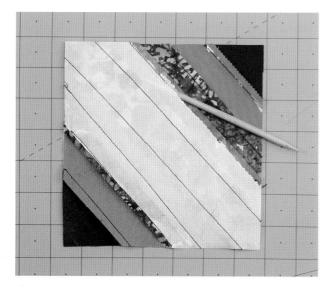

6. Carefully remove the foundation paper. The stitching enables the paper to tear easily along a seam line. Use a pencil, knitting needle, seam ripper or chopstick to help loosen the foundation. Tweezers also come in handy for grabbing small bits of paper.

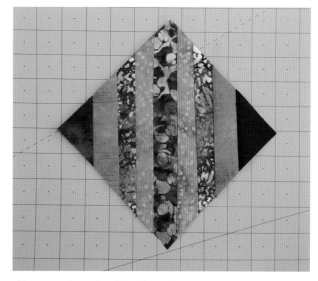

7. Pressing the block with Mary Ellen's Best Press™ or other starch helps the strings lay flat and helps a block maintain its shape.

Centered Seam Block

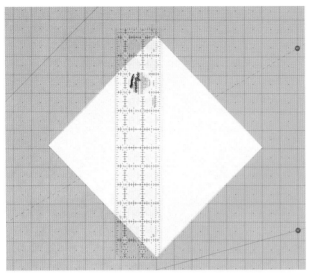

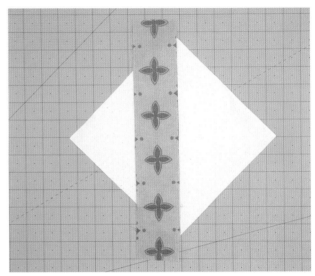

1. Select the correct size foundation. Using a pencil and a ruler, mark a ¼" (0.64cm) line to the right of the diagonal center of the foundation.

2. Place the first string right side up so that the right raw edge is lined up with the pencil line. Place a second string right side down on top of it, matching the right raw edges and sew in place.

3. Shown from the back, the seam is at the center of the block and the two strings divide the block.

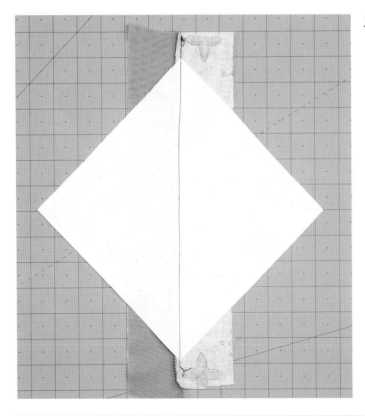

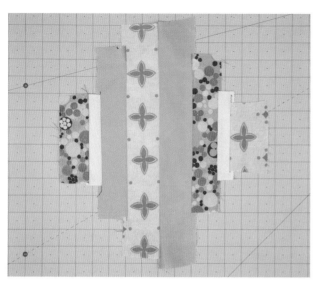

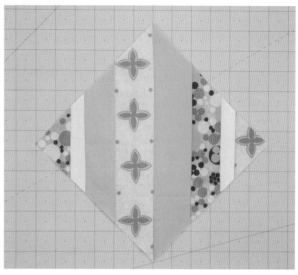

4. Open the string and press. Continue adding strings making sure the edges of the foundation are covered.

5. Turn the block over and trim, using the foundation as the trimming guide. Remove the paper backing from the block.

Two Half-square Triangles

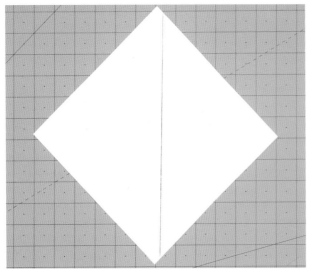

1. Select the paper foundation needed for the block. Draw a line ¼" (0.64cm) to the right of the diagonal center, as shown.

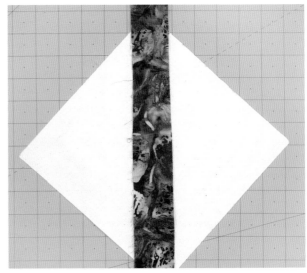

2. To center a string, place it right side up aligning the right raw edge along the line.

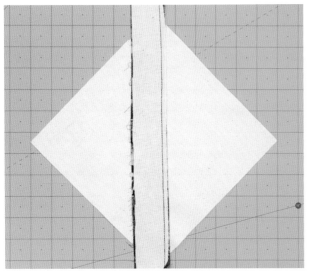

3. Put another string right side down on top of the first, matching the right raw edges. Sew with a ¼" (0.64cm) seam.

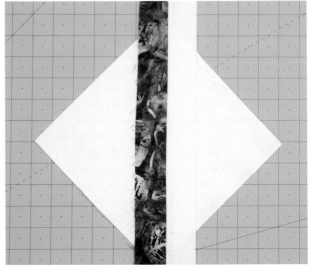

4. Open the string and press the seam.

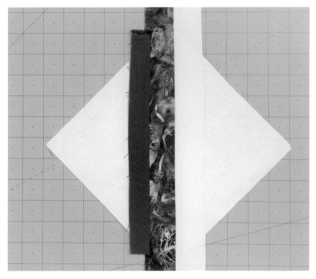
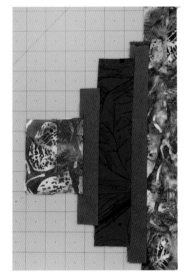
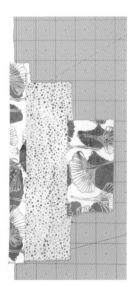

5. Continue adding strings, to the left and right of the center string.

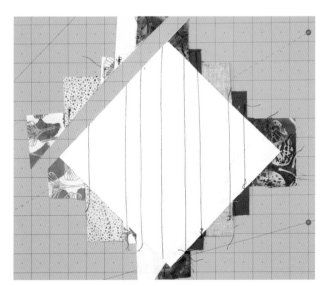

6. Turn the block over and trim, using the foundation as the trimming guide. Remove the paper backing and press the block.

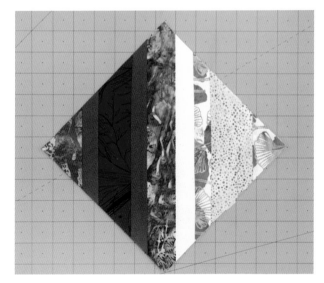

7. The seam of the first string set is centered through the diagonal middle of the block. Using dark strings on one side and light strings on the other, creates the two, half-square triangles.

Combining Half and Quarter-Square Triangles

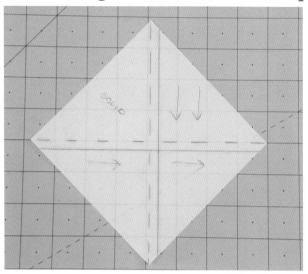

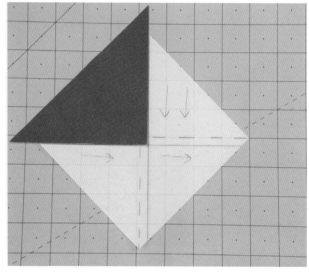

1. Mark the paper foundation ¼" (0.64cm) from the diagonal center in both directions. I find it helpful to mark each section with the color being used and the correct directions of the strings. Mark the sewing lines with dashes.

2. Align a background quarter-square triangle with the two drawn lines, as shown. Pin in place.

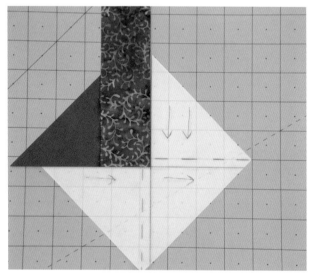

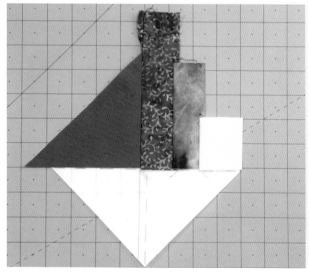

3. Place a string on the triangle, right sides together, matching up the right, raw edge. Sew in place. Do not sew past the drawn line. Open the string and press.

4. Continue adding strings until the foundation is covered. Press after each string as it's added.

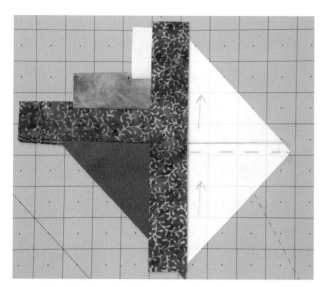

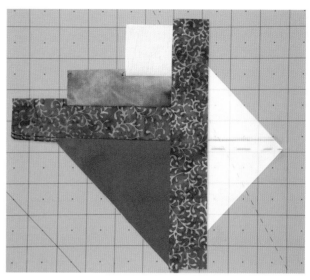

5. Turn the block a quarter-turn. Align a string with the edge of the drawn line and sew in place.

6. Open the string and press.

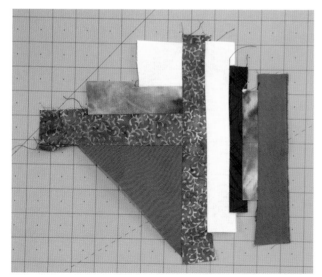

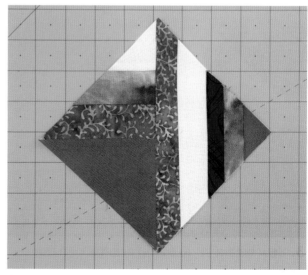

7. Continue adding strings until the half-square triangle background is covered.

8. Press the block carefully. Turn the block over and trim, using the paper foundation as a cutting guide. Remove the paper from the back.

Combining Two Directional Quarter-Square Triangles

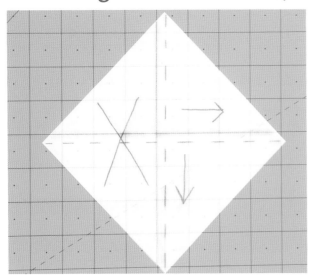

1. Mark a foundation paper with placement lines as shown. Use arrows to mark the direction the strings should go. The "X" indicates that nothing will be sewn to that part.

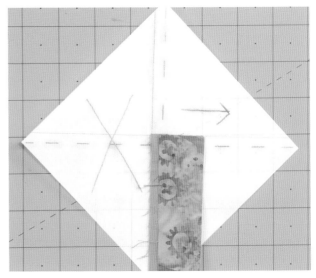

2. Align the edges of the first string, right side up, on the solid pencil lines. Pin a second string, right side down, aligning the right raw edge.

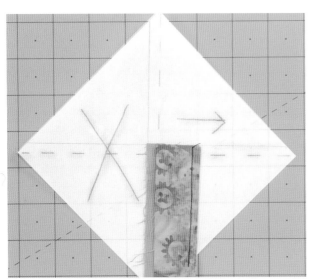

3. Sew with a ¼" (0.64cm) seam. Open the string and press.

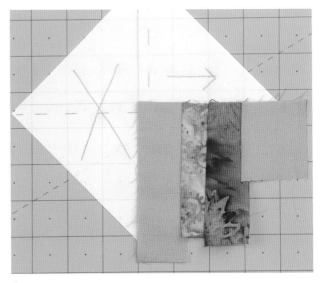

4. Continue adding strings to cover one quarter of the paper foundation as shown. Don't sew past the drawn line.

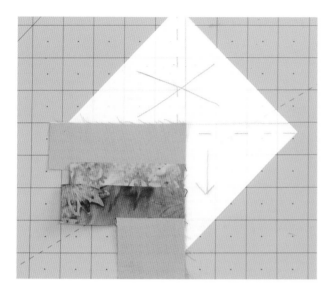

5. Turn the foundation ¼ turn, clockwise.

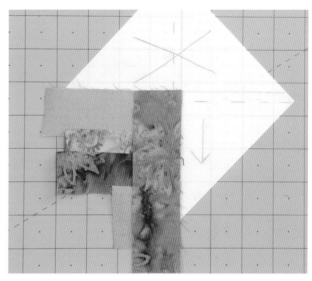

6. Align a string along the pencil lines and sew in place.

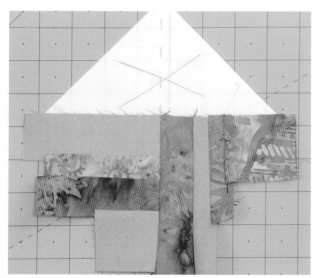

7. Continue adding strings to cover one quarter of the paper foundation as shown. Don't sew past the drawn line.

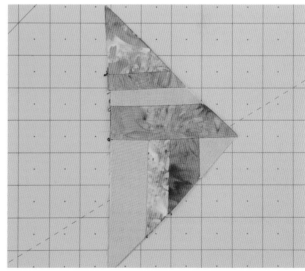

8. Press and remove the foundation paper from the back of the half-square triangle.

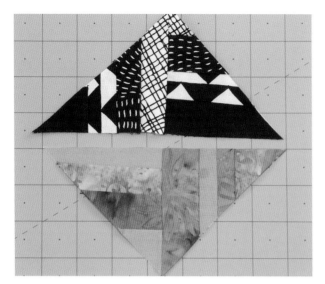

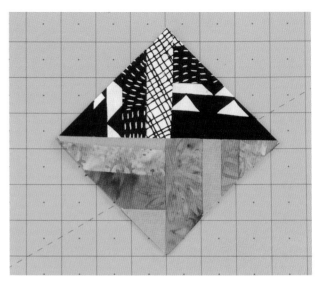

9. Make a second, contrasting half-square triangle, following steps 1–8, pages 22–23. Pay attention to the direction of the strips.

10. Sew the two contrasting half-square triangles together to make a quarter-square triangle.

Trimming and Removing Paper Foundation from Blocks

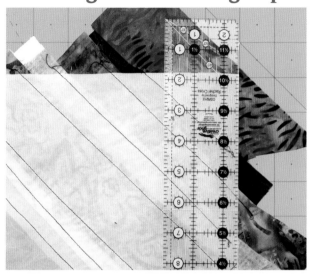

1. Use the edge of the foundation to align a ruler and trim a block.

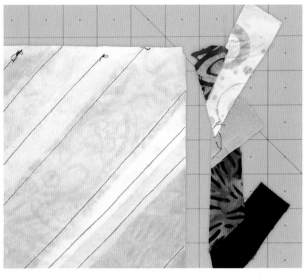

2. Trimmed blocks include a ¼" (0.64cm) seam allowance.

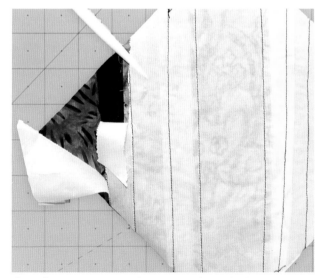

3. After trimming, the paper foundation is removed from the back of the block.

BACKGROUND FABRIC BLOCKS

Fabric is used when the background becomes a part of the block.

Single Half-Square Triangles

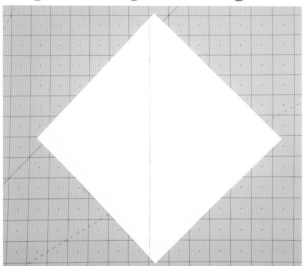

1. Using a pencil and ruler, draw a line ¼" (0.64cm) to the right of the diagonal center as shown.

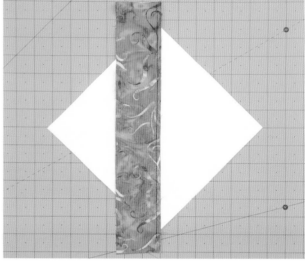

2. Place the first string right side down so that the right raw edge is lined up with the pencil line. Sew in place with a ¼" (0.64cm) seam.

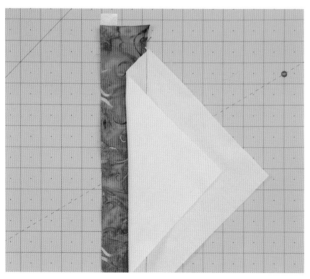

3. Fold the background out of the way and place a second string right side down on the first string, aligning the right raw edges. This photo shows the block from the back with fabric folded away.

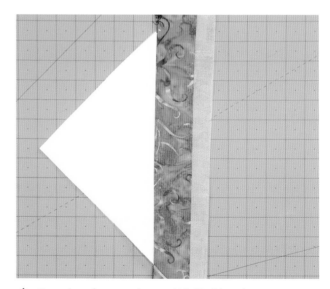

4. Sew in place using a ¼" (0.64cm) seam. Open the string and press. Fold the background fabric to the back.

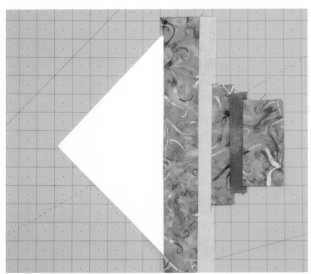

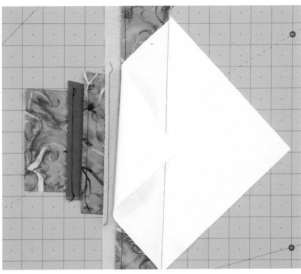

5. Continue adding strings, making sure the background fabric is folded out of the way of the strings.

6. Turn the block over and make sure that added strings completely cover the background. This background piece will be cut away.

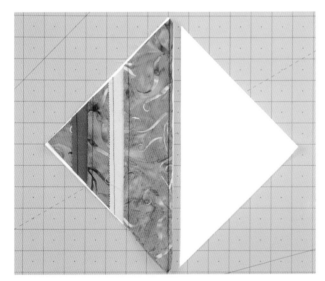

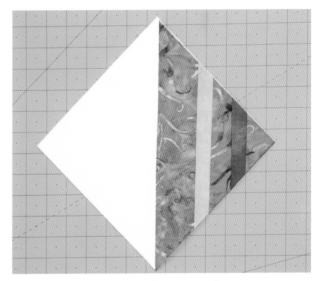

7. Trim the block, using the background fabric as a cutting guide. With the block facing up, fold the strings over the background and trim the fabric that is under the strings. Use the ¼" (0.64cm) seam as the cutting guide.

8. Fold the strings back over and press the block.

Half Covered Background Square

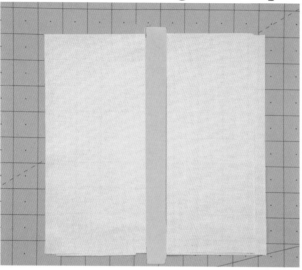

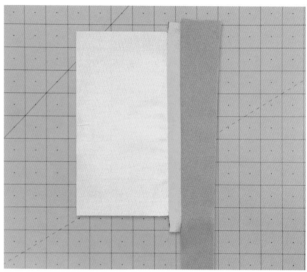

1. Select the correct size background block and mark a line ¼" (0.64cm) to the right of the background square. Place the first string right side down so that the right raw edge in lined up with the pencil line. Sew in place with a ¼" (0.64cm) seam.

2. Open the string and press. Fold the background out of the way and align a second string to the right raw edge of the first string. Sew in place.

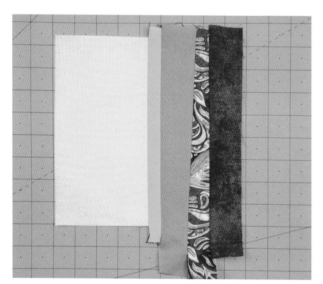

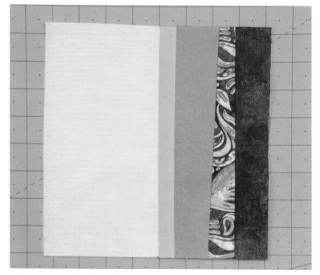

3. Continue adding strings, folding the background fabric out of the way as each string is added.

4. From the back, trim the block, using the background as the cutting guide. Trim the background fabric from under the strips, using the ¼" (0.64cm) seam line as a guide.

One Corner Covered Block

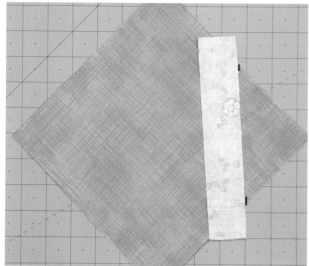

1. Select the correct size background block and mark the center right and bottom center of the square. Use the marks to place the first string and sew with a ¼" (0.64cm) seam.

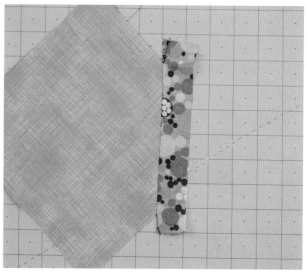

2. Open the string and press. Fold the background out of the way to keep from sewing through it as strings are added.

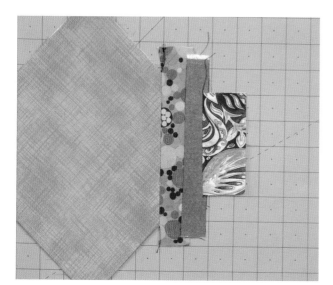

3. Continue adding and pressing strings to cover the corner of the block.

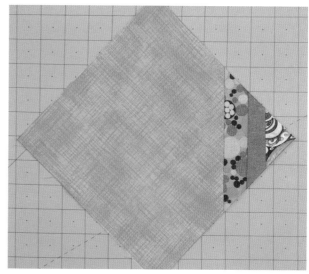

4. From the back, trim the block, using the sides as the cutting guide. Trim the fabric from under the strings

Four Corners Covered Block

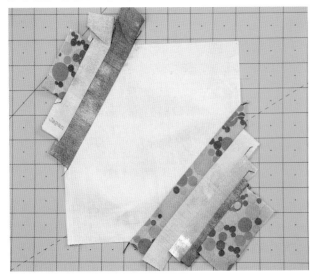

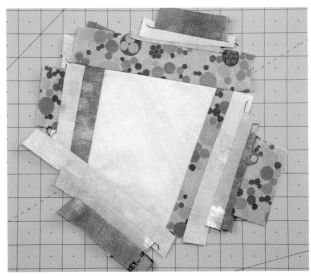

1. Cover the opposite corners of a fabric background, making sure to fold back the fabric as strings are added. Trim the background fabric, using the ¼" (0.64cm) seam as the cutting guide.

2. Cover the other two corners in the same manner.

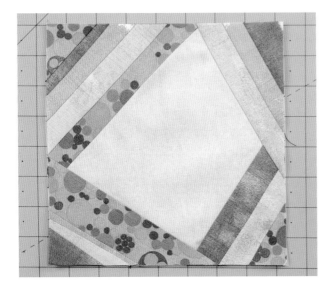

3. Trim the background fabric, using the ¼" (0.64cm) seam as the cutting guide.

Star Points

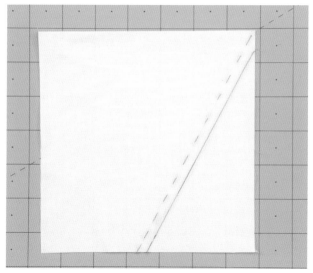

1. Mark the right side of the background to show where to place the first string. (After you've made a few blocks, you can probably skip this.) Mark from the top right to about the middle of the bottom of the block.

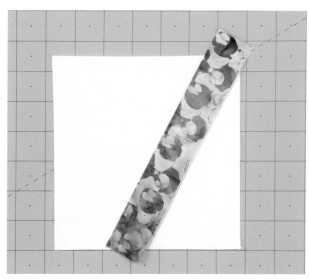

2. Place the first string right side down just to the left of the solid line. Sew in place with a ¼" (0.64cm) seam. Open the string and press.

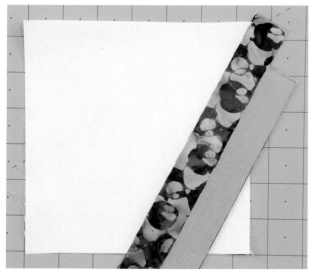

3. Place a second string right side down on the first string, aligning the right raw edges. Pull the background away from the strips. Sew in place using a ¼" (0.64cm) seam.

4. Open the string and press. Continue adding and pressing the strings. Fold the fabric out of the way as strings are added.

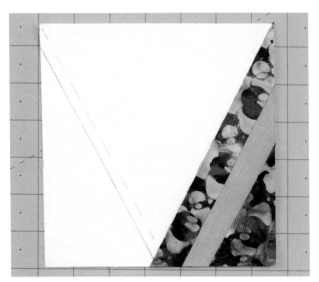

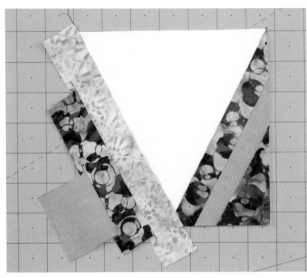

5. Fold the background fabric open as you add strings to make sure the entire background area is covered. Press the strings and trim the block, drawing another placement line on the left side of the block.

6. Add strings to cover the adjacent corner. Press and trim the strings, using the background fabric as the cutting guide.

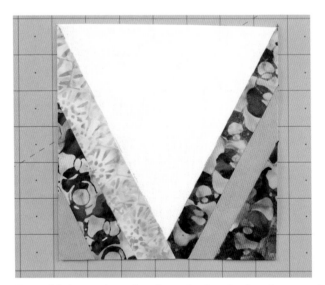

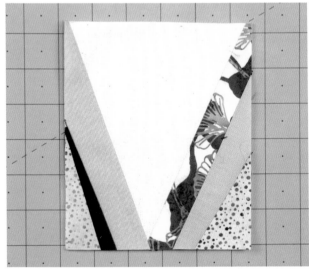

7. Fold the strings back and trim the background fabric along the ¼" (0.64cm) seam. This block is made on a square background fabric.

8. If you want more elongated star points, use rectangles and follow steps 1–7. The Starry, Starry Night Quilt, on page 86, combines square and rectangular star points. They don't need to be symmetrical.

ADDING INTEREST AND VARIATION TO BLOCKS

Changing the width and angle of strings and varying the value, print and color of fabric adds variety and interest to the blocks. Inserting crooked strings, disappearing strings, strings made from pieced sections, skinny strings, and selvage strings are specific techniques used to create wonky or irregular elements. These draw viewers in to look closely at the block sections.

Crooked Strings

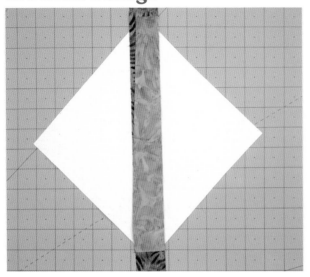

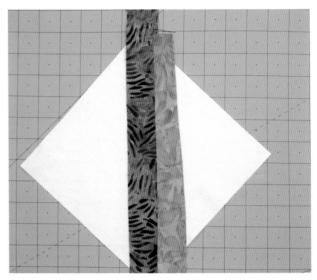

1. Select the foundation needed for the block. To center a string, place it right side up diagonally at about the center of the square. Place a crooked string right side down on top of the first, matching the right raw edges.

2. Sew the strings with a ¼" (0.64cm) seam, open the string and press.

3. Continue adding crooked strings, making sure they span the block edges.

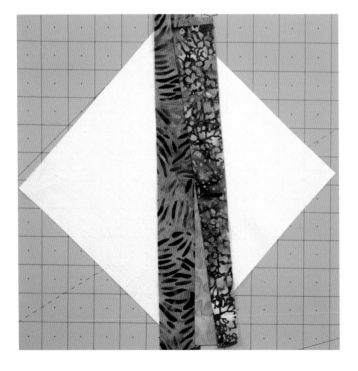

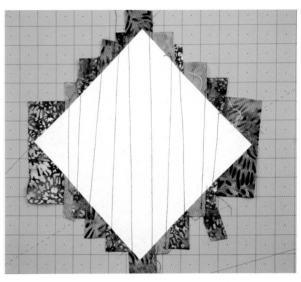

4. Alternate adding the strings on the left and right side of the center string.

5. Turn the block over and trim, using the foundation as the trimming guide.

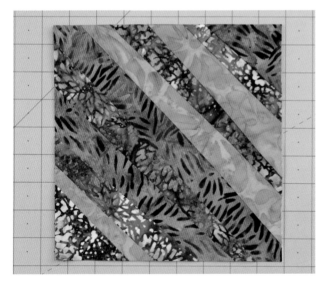

6. Remove the paper backing and press. This block may be used as a square or on point in a project.

Disappearing Strings

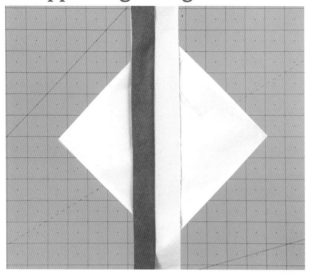

1. Referring to Diagonal Square Block, page 14, sew the first two strings to the foundation.

2. Place a fabric scrap or crooked string on one of the sewn strings, right sides together, as shown.

3. Sew the string in place and press open.

4. Continue adding strings until the foundation is covered. Trim the block to size using the foundation as a cutting guide. Remove the paper from the back of the block.

Above: Four Seasons of Trees Wall Hangings, pages 120-125, shows an example of how Disappearing Strings are used for branches.

Selvage Strings

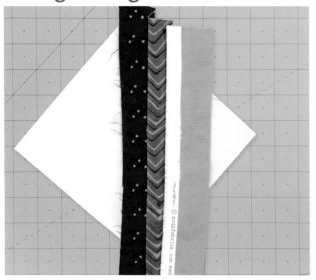

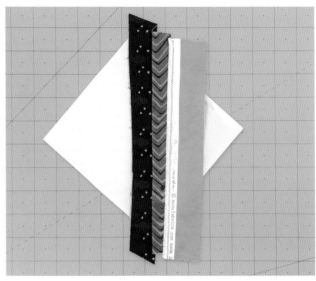

1. To add a selvage string, place it right side up on one of the previously sewn strings, overlapping the previous string by about ¼" (0.64cm). Pin the selvage in place.

2. Using a straight or narrow zigzag stitch, sew the strings together where they overlap. Sew as close as possible to the selvage edge.

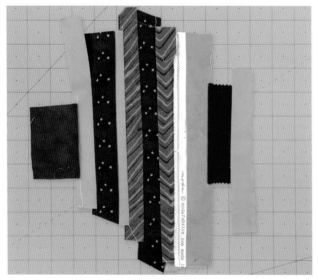

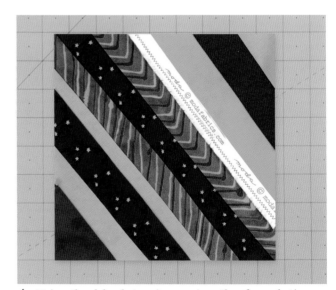

3. Continue adding strings until the foundation is covered.

4. Trim the block to size, using the foundation as a cutting guide. Remove the paper from the back of the block.

Pieced Strings

If a strip is too short to span the foundation, nothing says you can't piece it with other fabric to make it longer. The upper right corner shows two strings that were pieced just for this purpose.

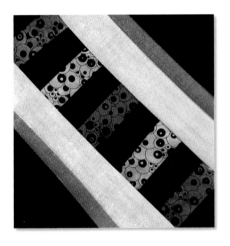

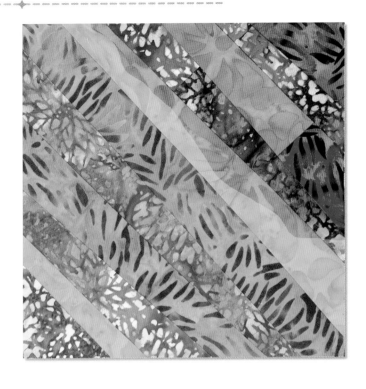

Skinny Strings

Adding a very skinny string is a nice variation when string widths are somewhat similar. Or, use up your skinny scraps to make a block.

SPECIALTY TECHNIQUES

These stringing techniques are used in four projects. Making Tree Panels is specific to Four Seasons of Tree Wall Hangings, page 120. Making Dresden Plate Sections is used in Dresden Plate Wall Hanging, page 98, and Dresden Plate Table Runner, page 104. Using Tulle for a Foundation is included in the border in String Churn Dash Quilt, page 68.

Making Tree Panels

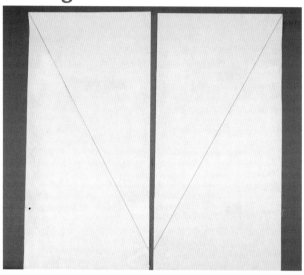

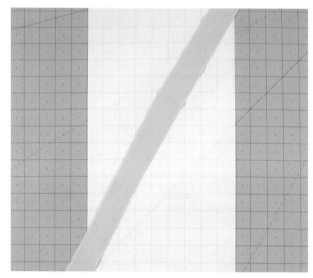

1. Cut two, 9" x 18" (22.86 x 45.72cm) paper foundations. Mark the paper as shown, drawing a pencil line from top corners to 1½" (3.81cm) of the bottom corners. Label the usable pieces as "top left" and "top right".

2. Place the first string, right side up, of the drawn line.

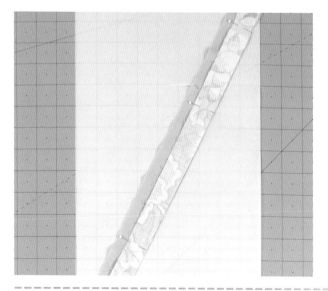

3. Align a second string, right side down, along the right, raw edge of the first string. Sew in place using a ¼" (0.64cm) seam.

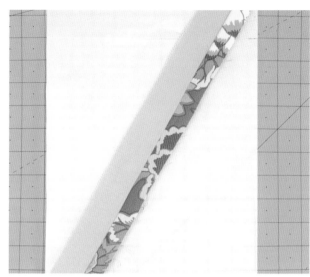

4. Open the string and press. Continue adding strings, to the left and right side of the foundation.

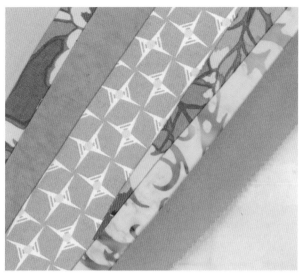

5. As you add strings, be sure to use crooked strings and disappearing strings to add interest to the trees.

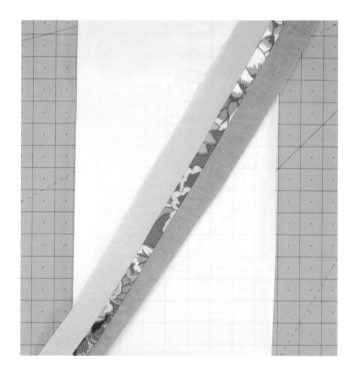

6. Crooked strings are added the same way as any other string. Align an edge with previously sewn string, making sure the string covers the foundation and sew in place.

Tip for Making Tree Panels:

Branches are bigger near the tree trunk and smaller as they extend out. Make some of your strips reflect this.

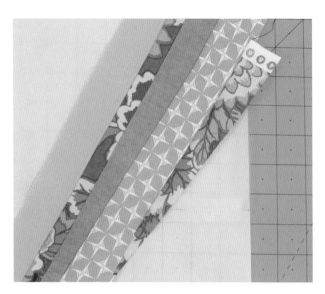

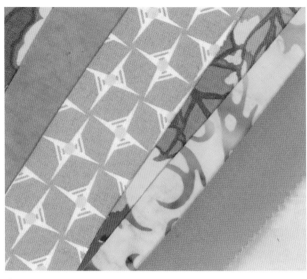

7. Add a short string to create a disappearing string.

8. Align another string to the edge of the disappearing string.

9. Continue adding strings until the paper foundation is covered.

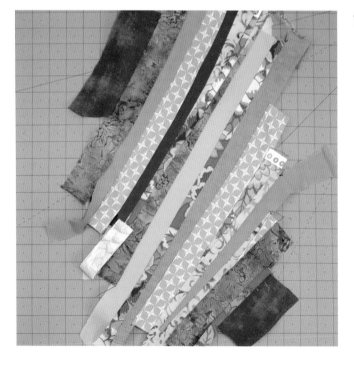

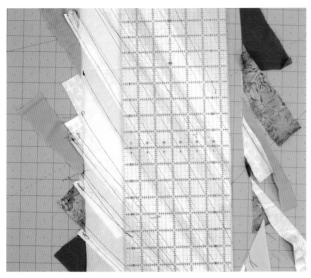

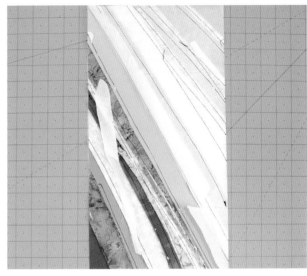

10. Trim the block using the paper foundation as a guide.

11. Carefully remove the paper from the back of the block.

12. Make the left tree block section in the same manner. Press both block sections. The two block sections do not need to be mirror images(or nearly mirror images) of each other as shown here.

Making Dresden Plate Sections

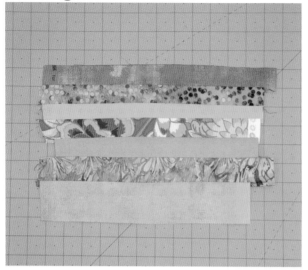

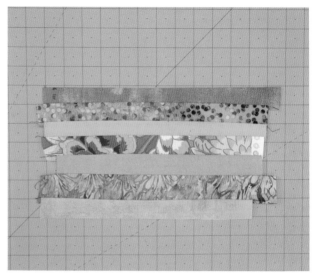

1. Sew together four to six, 11" (27.94cm) strings, mixing fabric and widths. You are making a piece of fabric for this technique.

2. Add strings until the set is at least 7" (17.78cm) wide. Trim to 7" (17.78cm) if the set is a bit bigger.

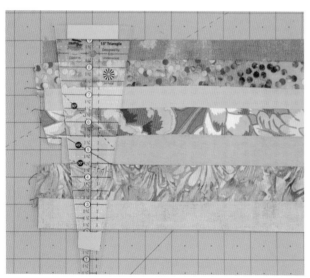

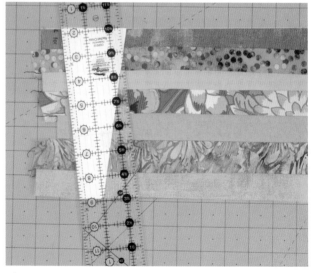

3. If you are using a 15° wedge template, place a piece of tape at the 2" (5.08cm) and 9" (22.86cm) lines of the ruler. This makes it easier to place the ruler as you cut sections.

4. If you are using the wedge paper template, (page 102), take care not to cut into the paper. Use the edge of a ruler to cut each side.

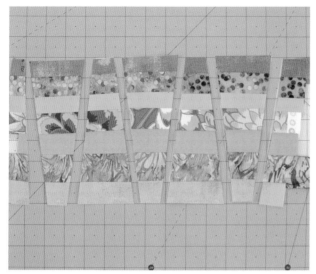

5. Cut wedge sections from the string set, flipping the ruler 180° across the set to cut four sections.

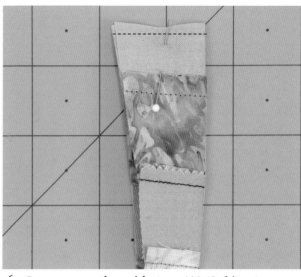

6. Sew across the wide top, ¼" (0.64cm) from the edge.

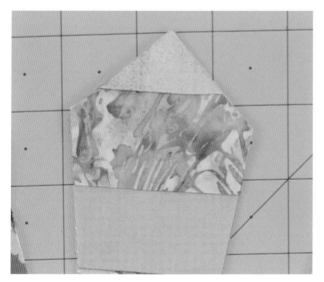

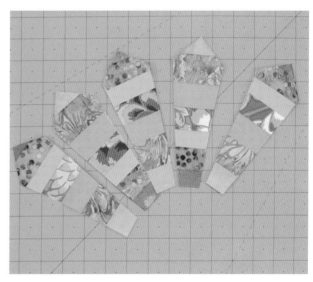

7. Turn the top, right side out, carefully pushing out the point, and press.

Using Tulle for a Foundation

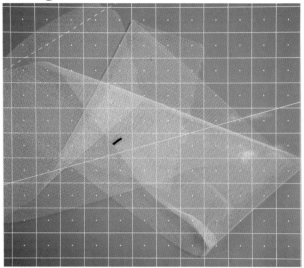

1. Cut a piece of 6" (15.24cm) tulle the length needed for your project. Determine which direction you want the strips to angle on your quilt borders. Find the center of the tulle strip and make a mark with pen or pencil.

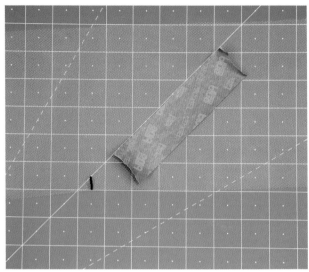

2. Use a ruler or cutting mat to determine a 45° angle. Use the marked center to place a piece of masking tape at that angle.

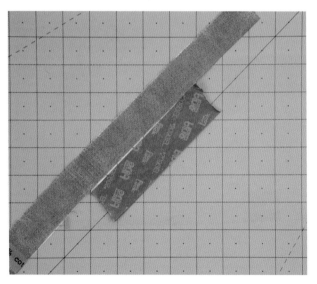

3. Place a string, right side up, along the edge of the tape.

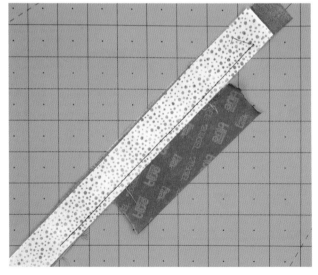

4. Put another string right side down on top of the first, matching the right raw edges. Sew with a ¼" (0.64cm) seam.

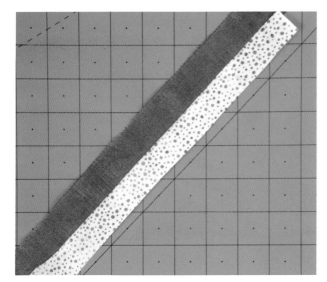

5. Remove the masking tape, open the string, and press.

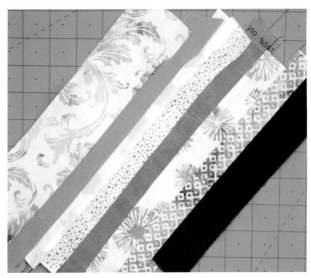

6. Continue adding strings to the left and right of the center string. Press before adding another string. The strings for a 6" (15.24cm) wide foundation, sewn at a 45° angle, need to be at least 10" (25.4cm) long. Very wide strings require more length.

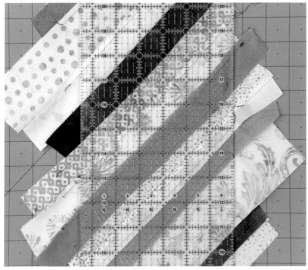

7. Continue adding strings to cover the length of the tulle foundation. Trim the sides, using the tulle as a cutting guide.

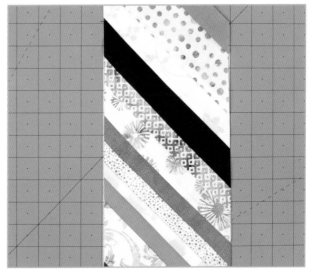

8. Trim the top and bottom of the string set after attaching it to the quilt.

String Quilt Projects

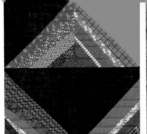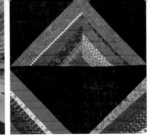

Night Flight Quilt

I liked the idea of interpreting geese flying in formation at night.
Light and dark values in the fabric create strong contrast in this quilt.

FINISHED QUILT SIZE APPROXIMATELY: 68" X 80" (152.40 X 203.20cm)
FINISHED BLOCK SIZE: 8" (20.32cm) SQUARE

MATERIALS

+ 5 yards (457.20cm) black solid or print for background fabric

+ ½ yard (45.72cm) assorted red solids or prints for strings

+ ¾ yard (68.58cm) assorted dark gray solids or prints for strings

+ ¾ yard (68.58cm) assorted medium gray solids or prints for strings

+ ¾ yard (68.58cm) assorted light gray solids or prints for strings

+ 5 yards (457.20cm) backing fabric

+ ⅝ yard (57.15cm) binding fabric

WOF = width of fabric

CUTTING INSTRUCTIONS

From the black solid or prints, cut:

(20) 8½" (21.59cm) x WOF strips. From the strips, cut:

(4) 8½" (21.59cm) squares from *each* strip for a total of 80 background squares

From the red, dark gray, medium gray and light gray solid or prints, cut:

Cut a variety of strings from 1" to 2¼" (2.5 to 5.76cm), cutting more 1¼" to 1¾" (2.5cm to 4.45cm) strings than others. Keeps strings sorted by color.

Since string sizes are varied, cut just enough strings to get started. Any uncut fabric and can be used for additional strings.

From the backing fabric cut:

(2) 90" (228.60cm) x WOF pieces

From the binding fabric cut:

(8) 2½" (6.35cm) x WOF strips

> This is a great opportunity to work with value (lightness and darkness) of gray fabrics.

CONSTRUCTING THE BLOCKS

This quilt requires (4) red, (6) dark gray, (6) medium gray, and (6) light gray flying geese blocks. Each flying geese block is made from (2) half-square triangle blocks. Refer to Single Half-Square Triangles, page 26, to make the blocks. The finished size of each flying geese block is 8" x 16".

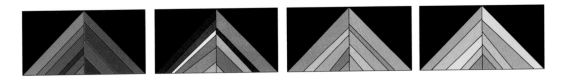

QUILT ASSEMBLY

1. Sew blocks together into rows as shown in the Quilt Assembly Diagram. Pay careful attention to the placement of the flying geese blocks. Press seams open.

Quilt Assembly Diagram

2. Sew the rows together. Press seams open.

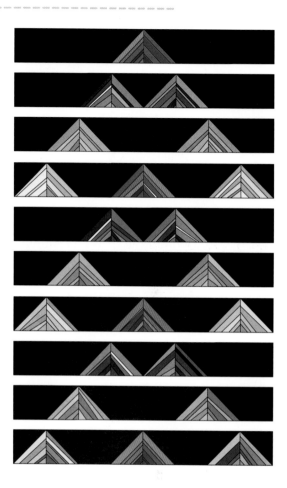

FINISHING THE QUILT

1. Trim the selvages from the (2) 90" (228.60cm) x WOF and sew the pieces together with a generous ¼" (0.64cm) seam. Press seam open.

2. Layer the backing, batting, and quilt top together and baste. Quilt as desired.

3. Sew the binding strips together on the diagonal to make one long strip. Press the strip wrong sides together. Sew the strip to the quilt top, matching the raw edges with the edge of the quilt. Fold the binding to the back, covering raw edges and hand stitch in place.

BONUS

Do you hate to waste fabric? Wondering what to do with the trimmed background triangles? Make some of these blocks to use on the back of the quilt.

1. Take (2) of the background half-square triangles that were trimmed off. Straighten the long edges on them if needed.

2. Find a leftover string and sew it to one of the half-square triangles. Press the seam.

3. Sew the other half square triangle to the other side of the string. Press the seam. Square up the block.

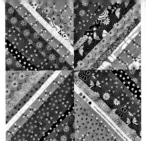

Carpenter Star Quilt

The Carpenter Star block relies on use of light (white), medium (gray prints), and dark values (dark teal and purple) for the design. Strings add variety and movement through the direction of the strings.Occasional white in the prints and selvages provide accents.

FINISHED QUILT SIZE APPROXIMATELY: 73" (185.42cm) SQUARE
FINISHED BLOCK SIZE: 8" (20.32cm) SQUARE

MATERIALS

♦ 3 yards (274.32cm) white fabric for background

♦ 6 fat quarters of dark value teals and purple prints for strings

♦ 6 fat quarters of medium gray value prints for strings

♦ (16) 8½" (21.59cm) paper foundations

♦ ½ yard (45.72cm) charcoal print for inner border

♦ ⅞ yard (80.01cm) medium gray print for outer border

♦ 4⅝ yards (422.91cm) backing fabric

♦ ⅝ yard (57.15cm) binding fabric

WOF = width of fabric

CUTTING INSTRUCTIONS

From the white background fabric, cut:
    (12) 8½" (21.59cm) x WOF strips. From the strips, cut:
    (4) 8½" (21.59cm) squares for a total of
    (48) background squares

From the fat quarter, teal and purple value prints, cut:
    1" to 2¼" (2.54 to 5.715cm) assorted width strings,
    cutting more 1¼" to 1¾" (3.18cm to 4.45cm)
    strings x WOF.

From the charcoal border print, cut:
    (8) 1¾" (4.45cm) x WOF strips

From the medium gray border print, cut:
    (8) 3½" (8.89cm) x WOF strips

From the backing fabric, cut:
    (2) 82" (208.28cm) x WOF strips

From the binding fabric, cut:
    (8) 2½" (6.35cm) x WOF strips

CONSTRUCTING THE BLOCKS

The Carpentar Star Quilt requires (16) white background squares, (16) medium half-square triangles on a background, (16) dark half square triangles on a background, (16) dark and medium half-square triangles on a foundation. Refer to Single Half-Square Triangles, page 26, and Two Half-Square Triangles, page 18.

QUILT ASSEMBLY

1. Arrange completed blocks using the diagram as a guide. Pay particular attention to the orientation of each block and the position of dark and medium value sections of each block. Sew blocks in each row together. Press seams open. Sew rows together, pressing seams open after adding each row.

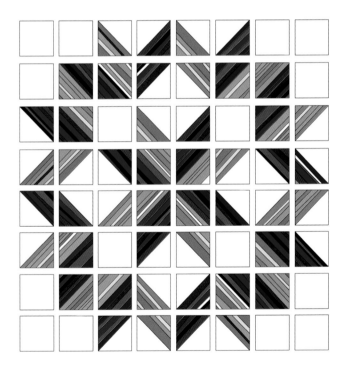

2. Add first border. Sew all 1¾" (4.45cm) border strips together into one long strip. Measure from side to side, cut top and bottom border strips to size and sew in place. Measure from top to bottom, cut side border strips to size and sew in place

3. Add second border. Sew all 3½" (8.89cm) border strips together into one long strip. Measure from side to side, cut top and bottom border strips to size and sew in place. Measure from top to bottom, cut side border strips to size and sew in place

4. Miter the corners if desired.

FINISHING THE QUILT

1. Trim the selvages from the (2) 82" (208.28cm) x WOF strips and sew together with a generous ¼" (0.64cm) as shown. Open and press.

2. Layer the backing, batting, and quilt top together and baste. Quilt as desired.

3. Sew the binding strips together using diagonal seams to create one continuous strip. Press the strip in half lengthwise, wrong sides together, and sew to the raw edge of the quilt top. Fold binding over raw edges and hand stitch in place.

Who says the back of a quilt needs to be one color or pattern? I keep the triangles that are cut away from background fabric, add strips to one long side of each triangle and make pieced sections for the backing. You can leave the back of your face up on your bed for a second quilt!

Circling Geese Quilt

For this quilt, small strings for the geese sections creates interest and variation. The red, square-in-a-square centers add a little zing to this formal quilt. The center block creates a focal point with its black background. The blocks are arranged in a Circle of Nine layout.

FINISHED QUILT SIZE APPROXIMATELY: 70" (177.80cm) SQUARE

MATERIALS

+ 8 light to medium fat quarters for flying geese background fabric

+ 1 dark taupe fat quarter for center flying geese block

+ 10 fat quarters of medium to dark taupe prints for main geese blocks

+ 6-8 fat eighths of assorted red print for square-in-a-square block centers

+ 7 assorted fat quarters of cream to beige prints for setting squares

+ ½ yard (45.72cm) red solid fabric for 1st border

+ 1⅛ yards (102.87cm) dark print for 2nd border

+ 4½ yards (411.48cm) backing fabric

+ ⅝ yard (57.15cm) binding fabric

WOF = width of fabric

CUTTING INSTRUCTIONS

Use the cutting diagram below to cut *each* of 9 background fat quarters.

    (1) 5½" x 18" (13.97 x 45.72cm) strip of fabric
    From the strip, cut:
    (3) 5½" x 5½" (13.97 x 13.97cm) squares

    (3) 3" x 18" (7.62 x 45.72cm) strips.
    From *each* of the strips, cut:
    (6) 3" x 3" (7.62 x 7.62cm) squares

From the remaining background, cut:

    (1) 5½" x 5½" (13.97 x 13.97cm) square

    (2) 3" x 3" (7.62 x 7.62cm) squares

From the red print fat eighths, cut:

¾" (1.905cm) to 1½" (3.81cm) assorted strings

Cutting diagram columns:
- 5½" x 18" sub-cut (3) 5½" squares
- 3" x 18" sub-cut (6) 3" squares
- 3" x 18" sub-cut (6) 3" squares
- 3" x 18" sub-cut (6) 3" squares
- 5½" x 5½"
- 3" x 3"
- 3" x 3"

Quilted by Joyce Brenner

Note: Do not cut all of the fabric until deciding your width of string preferences.

From *each* of 7 assorted cream to beige fat quarters, cut:
- (4) 8" (20.32cm) squares for a total of (28) setting squares

From the red solid border fabric, cut:
- (8) 1½" (3.81cm) x WOF strips

From the light gray print border fabric, cut:
- (8) 4½" (11.43cm) x WOF strips

From backing, cut:
- (2) 80" (203.20cm) x WOF pieces

From binding, cut:
- (8) 2½" (6.35cm) x WOF strips

MAKING THE FLYING GEESE BLOCKS

Make each flying block one at a time, using the same background fabric throughout the block. Refer to Single Half-Square Triangle instructions, page 26, to make the required half-square string triangles. Each flying geese block requires:

(4) 5½" (12.70cm) background squares

(4) Single Half-Square Triangle on a 3" (7.62cm) background (center contrast geese color)

(16) Single Half-Square Triangle on a 3" (7.62cm) background (geese color)

1. Sew the half-square triangles together to make the flying geese units. Press seams open.

Make 8   Make 4

2. Sew the geese units together in sets of two. Press seams open.

3. Lay out one center square, four geese blocks and four corner squares as shown.

4. Sew the blocks together in rows and pressing the seams open.

5. Sew the rows together, pressing the seams open.

6. Make a total of nine flying geese blocks.

QUILT ASSEMBLY

Referring to the Quilt Center Assembly Diagram, arrange the blocks into three sections, as shown. Sew the blocks together within each section, pressing the seams open,to make three rows. Sew the rows together, pressing the seams open, to finish the quilt top.

Quilt Center Assembly Diagram

ADDING THE BORDERS

As the borders are sewn to the quilt top, press the seams open.

1. For the first border sew the 1½" (3.81cm) red border strips together into one long strip.

2. Measure the quilt top from side to side. Cut top and bottom border strips to this size and sew in place.

3. Measure the quilt top from top to bottom. Cut the side border strips to size and sew in place.

4. For the second border sew the 4½"(11.43cm) border strips together into one long strip.

5. Measure the quilt top from side to side. Cut top and bottom border strips to size and sew in place.

6. Measure the quilt top from top to bottom. Cut the side border strips to this size and sew in place.

FINISHING THE QUILT

1. Trim the selvages from the (2) 40" (101.60cm) x WOF pieces and sew together, using a generous ¼" (0.64cm) seam. Press the seam open.

2. Layer the backing, batting, and quilt top together and baste. Quilt as desired.

3. Sew the binding strips together on the diagonal to make one long strip. Press the strip wrong sides together. Sew the strip to the quilt top, matching the raw edges with the edge of the quilt. Fold the binding to the back, covering raw edges and hand stitch in place.

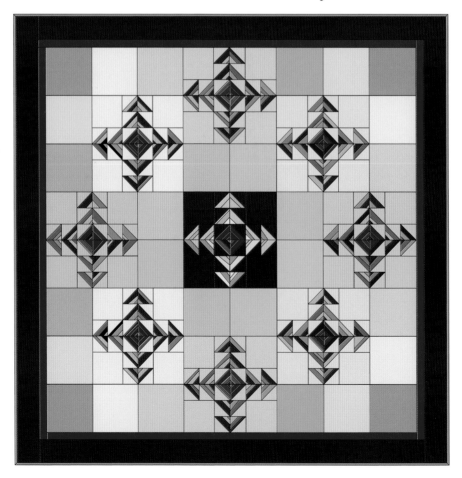

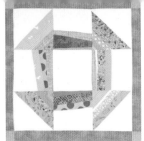

String Churn Dash Quilt

A solid white background sets off the blues and greens of this summery, Churn Dash quilt.
The border can be a solid color or you may choose to make a scrappy, string border.
Use up your scraps and don't worry if the colors aren't the same as those in the quilt.

FINISHED QUILT SIZE APPROXIMATELY: 77" X 94" (195.58 X 238.76cm)
FINISHED BLOCK SIZE: 15" (38.1cm) SQUARE

MATERIALS

✦ 4¼ yards (388.62cm) white fabric
  for background

✦ 5 yards (457.20cm) assorted fabric scraps
  for blocks

✦ 1⅜ yard (388.62cm) green marbled fabric
  for sashing

✦ ⅛ yard (34.29cm) light green marbled
  fabric for cornerstones

✦ 1¾ yards (160.02cm) fabric for borders
    *For optional string border:
    2½ (228.60cm) yards of fabric scraps
    6" (15.24cm) tulle on a spool or a roll
    of drawing paper to make 6" lengths
    of foundation paper for string borders

✦ 7¼ yards (662.94cm) backing fabric

✦ ¾ yard (68.58cm) binding fabric

WOF = width of fabric

CUTTING INSTRUCTIONS

From the white background fabric, cut:
  (26) 5½" (13.97cm) x WOF strips. From the strips, cut:
  (7) 5½" (13.97cm) squares for a total of
  (180) squares

From the assorted fabric scraps, cut:
  ¾" to 1½" (1.91 to 3.81cm) assorted strings

From the green marbled fabric, cut:
  (3) 15½" (39.37cm) x WOF strips of fabric.
  From the strips, cut:
  (49) 2" x 15½" (5.08 x 39.37cm) strips

From the light green marbled fabric, cut:
  (2) 2" (5.08cm) x WOF strips. From the strips, cut:
  (30) 2" (5.08cm) squares

From the border fabric, cut:
  (9) 6" (15.24cm) x WOF strips

If making optional string border
From fabric scraps, cut:
  ¾" to 1½" (1.91 to 3.81cm) x 10" (25.40cm) strings

From the backing fabric, cut:
  (3) 85" (215.90cm) x WOF pieces

From the binding fabric, cut
  (10) 2½" (6.35cm) strips

CONSTRUCTING THE BLOCKS

The Churn Dash block is a nine patch block. Refer to Half Covered Background Square, page 28 and Single Half-Square Triangles, page 26.

1. Each block requires:

(4) half-covered background squares

(4) single half-square triangles for the corners

(1) plain center square

2. Lay out the squares as shown. Sew the squares together in rows and press seams open. Sew the rows together and press seams open to make 20 Churn Dash blocks.

Make your blocks scrappy in the same color value, or position the same fabric string in each square, as shown, in the far left block below.

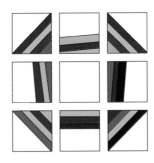

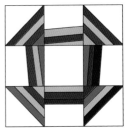

Make 20

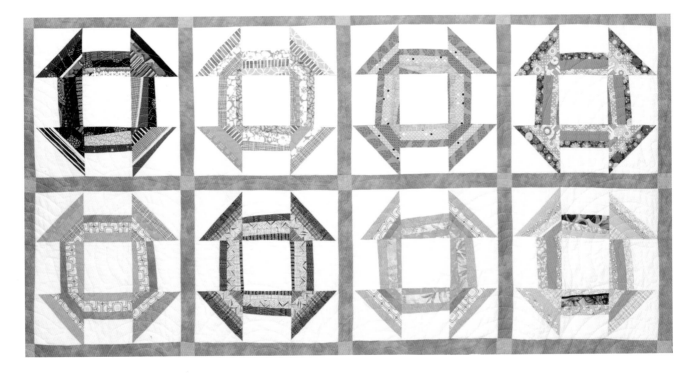

SASHING STRIPS

Sew (5) 2" cornerstones to (4) 2" X 15½" rectangles to make a row of sashing. Make (6) rows of sashing.

Make 6

QUILT CENTER ASSEMBLY

1. Lay out the blocks and 2" x 15½" (5.08 x 39.37cm) sashing strips, as shown.

2. Sew the blocks and sashing strips together to make rows.

3. Make (5) rows of (4) blocks.

4. Sew the six sashing rows to the quilt block rows to finish the quilt center.

ADDING THE BORDERS

The finished quilt size will be about 77" x 94" (195.58 x 238.76cm) after adding borders. The string borders are made longer to allow for mitering the corners. The borders use strings sewn at about a 45° angle to the foundation length. Strings need to be a minimum of 10" (25.40cm) long. Refer to Using Tulle for a Foundation, page 46.

1. Cut (2) 6" x 85" (15.24 x 215.90cm) foundations for the top and bottom border sections. 6" (15.24cm) tulle on a spool was used for this quilt.

2. Cut (2) 6" x 100" (15.24 x 254cm) foundations for the side border sections.

3. Work with one border piece at a time. If you are using a paper foundation, use a pencil and ruler to draw a 45° line near the center of the foundation, choosing which way you want your strings to go.

   Mark the angle with a piece of masking tape. Begin sewing strings to the foundation using the line as a guide, then remove the masking tape. Strings must be long enough to cover the edges of the foundation when turned and pressed. Very wide strings will require longer lengths. Continue adding strings, and press before adding another string. Continue until the foundation is covered. The tulle is left in place. Trim the border sections to a 6" width.

4. Complete the other three border sections the same way.

5. Mark the center of the quilt top and the center of a 6" x 85" (15.24 x 215.90cm) top border strip. Align the center marks and pin the border strip right side down on the quilt top.

6. Sew the border to the quilt top beginning and ending ¼" (0.64cm) from each corner.

7. Repeat steps 5–6 with the bottom and side borders.

8. Lay the quilt top right side up on an ironing board. Extend the borders so the vertical border strip overlays the horizontal one.

9. Fold the vertical border strip at a 45° angle and press.

10. Fold the quilt top, right sides together, on the diagonal so the edges of the two border strips align. Pin the borders together along the creased line.

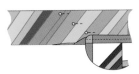

11. Sew on the creased line to make the mitered seam.

12. Trim the seam to ¼" (0.64cm) and press open.

13. Repeat on the remaining corners.

14. 14. Stitch ¼" (0.64cm) from the edge on all sides of the quilt to hold the border strings in place while the project is being quilted.

FINISHING THE QUILT

1. Trim the selvages from the three 40" X 85" (101.60 x 215.90cm) backing pieces and sew together using a generous ¼" (0.64cm) seam. Press seams open.

2. Layer the backing, batting, and quilt top together and baste. Quilt as desired.

3. Sew the binding strips together on the diagonal to make one long strip. Press the strip wrong sides together. Sew the strip to the quilt top, matching the raw edges with the edge of the quilt. Fold the binding to the back, covering raw edges and hand stitch in place.

Shoo Fly Quilt

These Shoo Fly blocks go together quickly, and the use of narrow sashing strips on two sides of each block adds interest to the overall layout of the quilt.

FINISHED QUILT SIZE APPROXIMATELY: 75" X 91" (190.5 X 231.14cm)

MATERIALS

+ 6 yards (548.64cm) blue fabric for block backgrounds, sashing, and quilt borders

+ 20 assorted pastel print and solid fat quarters for blocks and borders

+ 7½ yards (685.80cm) backing fabric

+ ¾ yard (68.58cm) binding fabric

+ (20) 5½" (13.97cm) square paper foundations for block centers

WOF = width of fabric

CUTTING INSTRUCTIONS

From the blue fabric, cut:

(24) 5½" (13.97cm) x WOF strips. From *each* strip, cut: (7) 5½" (13.97cm) squares for a total of 164

(20) 1¾" x 15½" (4.45 x 39.37cm) block sashing strips

(20) 1¾" x 16¾" (4.45 x 42.55cm) block sashing strips

(3) 2" (5.08cm) x WOF strips. From the strips, cut: (5) 2" x 20" (5.08 x 50.8cm) strips

(3) 3" (7.62cm) x WOF strips. From the strips, cut: (5) 3" x 20" (7.62 x 50.8cm) strips

(3) 3½" (8.89cm) x WOF strips. From the strips, cut: (5) 3½" x 20" (8.89 x 50.8cm) strips

(3) 4" (10.16cm) x WOF strips. From the strips, cut: (5) 4" x 20" (10.16 x 50.8cm) strips

(3) 4½" (11.43cm) x WOF strips. From the strips, cut: (5) 4½" x 20" (11.43 x 50.8cm) strips

From the 20 assorted pastel print fat quarters, cut:

(5) 4" x 20" (10.16 x 50.8cm) strips

(5) 3" x 20" (7.62 x 50.8cm) strips

(5) 2½" x 20" (6.35 x 50.8cm) strips

(5) 2" x 20" (5.08 x 50.8cm) strips

(5) 1½" x 20" (3.81 x 50.8cm) strips

1" to 1¾" (2.54 to 4.45cm) x 20" (50.8cm) strips from remaining fat quarter fabric

From the backing fabric, cut:

(3) 90" (228.6cm) x WOF pieces

From the binding fabric, cut:

(10) 2½" (6.35cm) x WOF strips

CONSTRUCTING THE BLOCKS

1. This is a nine patch block. Strings are sewn directly to a 5½"
(13.97cm) background fabric square to make 80, half-square triangles,
(4) for each corner of a block. Refer to Single Half-Square Triangles,
page 26.

2. After sewing strings to half of the background
fabric, trim each block using the background as
a guide. Trim away background fabric under the
string section.

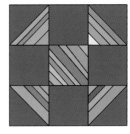

3. Refer to Diagonal Square Block, page 14, use
a 5½" (13.97cm) paper foundation to make a
diagonal square string block for each center
block. Trim the block, and remove paper.

4. Lay out 9 squares, as shown, for each block.
Sew the blocks into rows. Press seams open.
Sew the rows together, and press seams open.

   Make 20, 15½" (39.37cm) blocks.

Make 20

SASHING

1. Stack all the blocks so that the center strings are
oriented the same way.

2. Sew a 1¾" x 15½" (4.45 x 39.37cm) blue sashing
strip to the top of each block.

3. Sew a 1¾" x 17" (4.45 x 43.18cm) blue sashing
strip to the left side of (10) blocks and the right
side of (10) blocks.

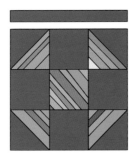

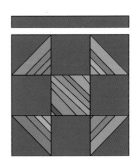

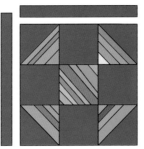

Make 10

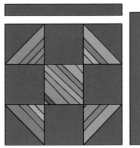

Make 10

CENTER QUILT TOP ASSEMBLY

1. Arrange the blocks, as shown in the Center Quilt Top Assembly Diagram. Rotate the blocks as needed to achieve the layout, keeping all the diagonal square centers oriented the same.

2. Sew the blocks together in rows. Press the seams.

3. Sew the rows together. Press the seams.

Center Quilt Top Assembly Diagram

MAKING AND ADDING THE BORDERS

The 5" (12.70cm) Crooked Stair Step borders are made from strip sets. Strip sets are made; cut into a variety of widths; and sewn back together. Corner border sections are made separately.

1. Make (4) border corner half square triangle sections with light strings using 5½" (13.97cm) squares of blue border fabric as background. Refer to Single Half-Square Triangles, page 26. Set aside.

Make 4

2. Make (5) each of the following strip sets using the assorted fat quarter strips and dark background fabric strips.

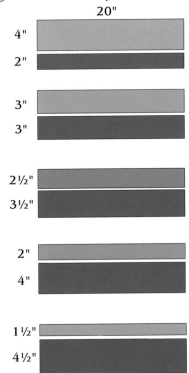

3. Cut the strip sets into segments of varying widths:
   1½" (3.81cm),
   2" (5.08cm),
   2½" (6.35cm)
   3" (7.62cm)

4. Sew approximately (10) segments into sections. Mix the segment sizes and fabrics, trim to 5½" (13.97cm).

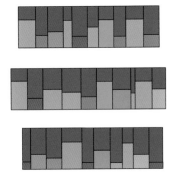

5. Measure the quilt center from top to bottom to determine the length of the side borders.

   Sew enough border sections together to fit the sides. Sew the borders in place and trim, if necessary.

6. Measure the quilt center between the side borders. Sew enough border sections together to fit the top and bottom of the quilt between the borders.

7. Sew a corner block from step 1, page 76, to each end of the top and bottom borders. Sew the borders in place.

FINISHING THE QUILT

1. Trim the selvages from the (3) 90" (228.60cm) x WOF pieces and sew together using a generous ¼" (0.64cm) seam. Press seams open.

2. Layer the backing, batting, and quilt top together and baste. Quilt as desired.

3. Sew the binding strips together on the diagonal to make one long strip. Press the strip wrong sides together. Sew the strip to the quilt top, matching the raw edges with the edge of the quilt. Fold the binding to the back, covering raw edges and hand stitch in place.

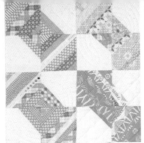

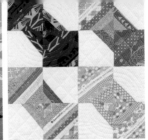

Rainbow Sherbet Quilt

These Bow Tie string blocks are made from eight different color groups against a white-on-white background fabric. A fellow quilter said the color palette reminded her of rainbow sherbet, with fruity colors of lime, raspberry, orange and lemon. This is a fairly easy quilt to make. Feel free to use your own color choices if Rainbow Sherbet isn't your taste!

FINISHED QUILT SIZE APPROXIMATELY: 72" X 88" (182.88 X 223.52cm)
FINISHED BLOCK SIZE: 8" (20.32cm) SQUARE

MATERIALS

+ 2¾ yards (251.46cm) white fabric for background

+ ⅜ yard (34.29cm) white fabric for inner border

+ 8 assorted fat quarters or scraps for each of 8 colorways for strings and borders

+ (160) 4½" (11.43cm) paper foundations

+ 5½ yards (502.92cm) backing fabric

+ ¾ yard (68.58cm) binding fabric

WOF = width of fabric

CUTTING INSTRUCTIONS

From the white background fabric, cut:
  (20) 4½" (11.43cm) x WOF strips. From the strips, cut:
    (8) 4½" (11.43cm) squares for a total of 160

From the assorted fat quarters or scraps, cut:
  1" to 2" (2.54 to 5.08cm) strings, cutting more 1¼" to 1¾" (3.16 to 4.45cm) strings than others

  You can cut 1½" (3.81cm) selvage strings before cutting other strings. I used them a lot in the blocks.

  Keep strings of each color group separate

  Note: Do not cut all the fabric for blocks at one time. Cut about ⅓ of each fat quarter into strings and cut more as needed. Some fabric will be needed for borders.

From the white border fabric, cut:
  (9) 1½" (3.81cm) x WOF strips

From the backing fabric, cut:
  (2) 99" (251.46cm) x WOF pieces

From the binding fabric, cut:
  (9) 2½" (6.35cm) x WOF strips

CONSTRUCTION OF THE BLOCKS

Each Bow Tie block requires (2) Diagonal Square Blocks, page 14, and (2) One Covered Corner Block, page 29.

1. Working with one color group, make two of each square, as shown, and sew together to make a block.

2. Make (80) blocks, about 10 in each of colorways. Add occasional crooked strings, skinny strings, and selvage strings to add interest to your blocks.

Make 80

QUILT CENTER ASSEMBLY

1. Position the (80) blocks in a pleasing layout, of 10 rows of 8 blocks.

2. Sew the blocks together in rows. Press the seams.

3. Sew the rows together, and press the seams, to finish the quilt center.

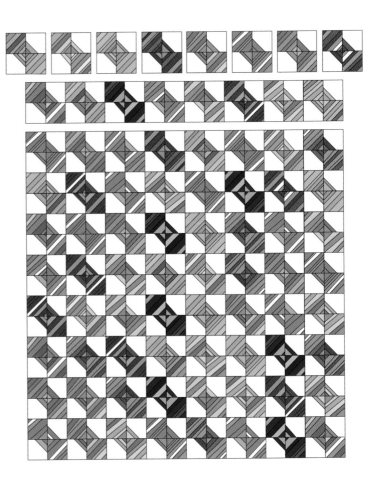

MAKING THE BORDERS

1. For the inner border, sew the (9) 1½" (3.81cm) white border strips together into one long strip.

2. Cut 2" (5.08cm) x WOF strips from the fat quarter fabrics left from making the blocks. Sub-cut the strips into varying lengths from 4" to 10" (10.16 to 25.40cm).

3. Sew the strips end to end, into long sections, varying the fabrics and lengths.

4. Make (4) sections, approximately 76" (193.04cm) long, and (4) sections approximately 92" (233.68cm) long. The extra length of the borders is for mitering the corners.

5. Sew (2) 76" (193.04cm) strips together lengthwise to create a strip that is 3½" x 76" (8.89 x 193.04cm). Repeat with the other two 76" (193.04cm) strips.

6. Sew (2) 92" (233.68cm) strips together lengthwise to create a strip that is 3½" x 92" (8.89 x 233.68cm) long. Repeat with the other (2) 92" (233.68cm) strips.

7. Sew a 1½" (3.81cm) white strip to one side of each of the (4) border sections

ADDING THE BORDERS

1. For the top and bottom border, mark the center of the quilt and the center of the 76" (193.04cm) border strips.

2. Align the centers and sew the borders in place, starting and ending ¼" (0.64cm) from each corner.

3. Repeat steps 1 and 2 with the 92" (233.68cm) border strips for the side borders of the quilt.

MITERING THE BORDER CORNERS:

1. Lay the quilt top right side up on an ironing board. Extend the borders so the vertical border strip overlays the horizontal one.

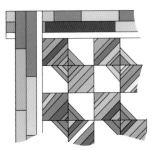

2. Fold the vertical border strip at a 45° angle and press.

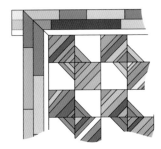

3. Fold the quilt top, right sides together, on the diagonal so the edges of the two border strips align. Pin the borders together along the creased line.

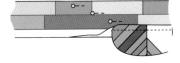

4. Sew on the creased line to make the mitered seam.

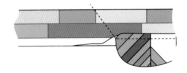

5. Trim the seam to ¼" (0.64cm) and press open.

6. Repeat on the remaining corners.

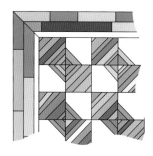

FINISHING THE QUILT

1. Trim the selvages from the (2) 99" (251.46cm) x WOF strips and sew the pieces together with a generous ¼" (0.64cm) seam. Open the seam and press.

2. Layer the backing, batting, and quilt top together and baste. Quilt as desired.

3. Sew the binding strips together using diagonal seams to create one continuous strip. Press the strip in half lengthwise, wrong sides together, and sew to the raw edge of the quilt top. Fold binding over raw edges and hand stitch in place.

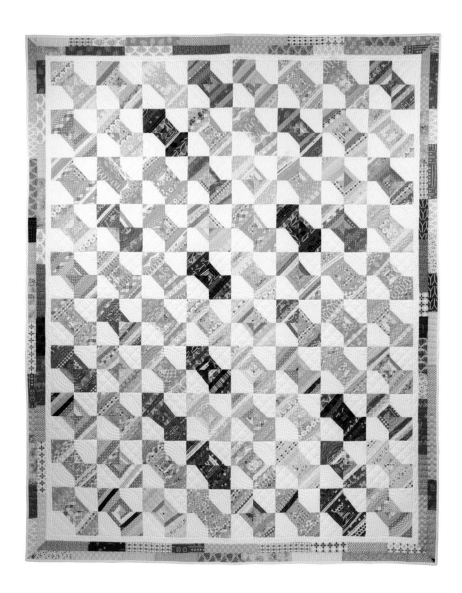

Starry, Starry Night Quilt

In this quilt, colorful stars radiate across the blackness of an evening sky, showing the true colors of millions of stars we always see as white. Star points border the blocks, scattering rays of star light.

FINISHED QUILT SIZE APPROXIMATELY: 70" X 80" (177.80 X 203.20cm)
FINISHED BLOCK SIZE: 15" (38.10cm) SQUARE

MATERIALS

✦ 5 yards (457.20cm) of background fabric for blocks and borders

✦ ⅜ yard (34.29cm) of assorted fabric pieces of 16 different block colors for strings, blocks, and borders

✦ 5 yards (457.20cm) backing fabric

✦ ⅝ yard (57.15cm) binding

WOF = width of fabric

CUTTING INSTRUCTIONS

For more elongated star points, use rectangles and refer to steps 1–7, Star Points, pages 31–32.

From the background and border fabric, cut:
(24) 5½" (13.97cm) x WOF strips
(168) 5½" (13.97cm) squares (7 from *each* strip)
(144 for blocks, 24 for side borders)
(4) 10½" (26.67cm) x WOF
(28) 5½" x 10½" (13.97 x 26.67cm) pieces
(7) from *each* strip

From the assorted fabric pieces, cut:
1½" (3.81cm) strings

From the backing fabric, cut:
(2) 90" (228.6cm) x WOF pieces

From the binding fabric, cut:
(9) 2½" (6.35cm) x WOF strips

> Starry, Starry Night is the perfect quilt to use your leftover fabrics or scraps from your stash.

CONSTRUCTING THE BLOCKS

This is a nine patch star block. You will be using strings to cover parts of the background fabrics to make a star.

1. Lay out (9) 5½" (13.97cm) background squares for a block. It is helpful to put sections in place as they are constructed to assure that the block is being built correctly.

2. Each block requires: (4) plain corner sections; (4) star point sections; (1) middle section with Four Corner Covered Block, page 30.

3. Refer to Star Points, page 31, to make a star point section. Use a 5½" (13.97cm) background fabric square for each star point block section. Cover one side of the star and trim it before starting the other star point. Vary the star point sections to make the blocks more interesting.

4. Sew the block sections together. Make a total of 16 blocks.

Note: Pressing seams open minimizes the bulky seam sections that can result from multiple strings in the seam allowance.

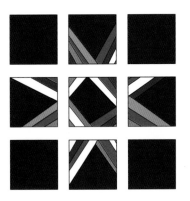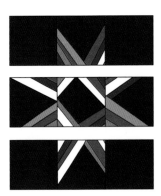

CONSTRUCTING THE BORDER

1. For the side borders, construct (24) blocks for side borders (12 for each side) using 5½" (13.97cm) square background pieces. These are made the same way the star points sections were constructed. However, rather than using the same color within each block, block point colors match the blocks next to them (See quilt layout and photo). It is best to make these blocks one at a time, moving from left to right, changing the colors.

2. Sew the side border sections together using a ¼" seam allowance. Press seams open.

3. For the top and bottom borders, construct (24) blocks for top and bottom borders (12 for the top and 12 for the bottom) using the 5½" x 10½" (13.97 x 26.67cm) background pieces. These are made the same way the star points sections were constructed. However, rather than using the same color within each block, block point colors match the blocks next to them (See quilt layout and photo). Make these blocks one at a time, moving from left to right, changing the colors. Sew the top and bottom border sections together using a ¼" (0.64cm) seam allowance. Press seams open.

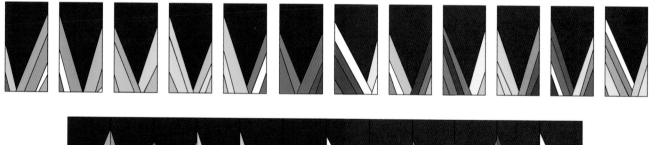

4. Four 5½" x 10½" (13.97 x 26.67cm) background pieces are used in the corners. Corners look best when adjacent points used the same color. Sew the 5½" x 10½" (13.97 x 26.67cm) background pieces to each side of the top and bottom border.

QUILT TOP ASSEMBLY

1. Layout the quilt to get a pleasing arrangement of blocks.

2. Sew the blocks together in rows. Press seams open. Sew the rows together to complete the quilt center.

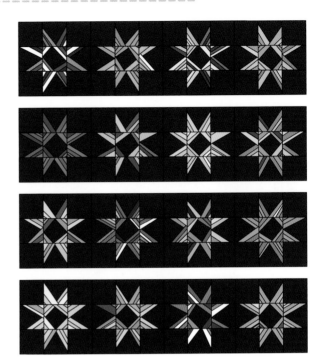

3. Sew the side borders to the quilt top. Press seams open. Sew the top and bottom borders to the quilt top. Press seams open.

FINISHING THE QUILT

1. Trim the selvages from the (2) 90" (228.60cm) x WOF pieces and sew together using a generous ¼" (0.64cm) seam. Press seams open.

2. Layer the backing, batting, and quilt top together and baste. Quilt as desired.

3. Sew the binding strips together on the diagonal to make one long strip. Press the strip wrong sides together. Sew the strip to the quilt top, matching the raw edges with the edge of the quilt. Fold the binding to the back, covering raw edges and hand stitch in place.

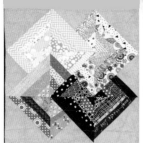

Card Trick Table Topper

A light gray blender fabric provides the background, while four colors of strings are used to make the blocks: white prints with a little black, pink prints, gray prints and black prints. This creates the illusion of cards nested with each other.

FINISHED TABLE TOPPER SIZE APPROXIMATELY: 45" X 55" (114.30 X 139.70cm)
FINISHED BLOCK SIZE: 15" (38.10cm) SQUARE

MATERIALS

+ 1 yard (91.44cm) light gray fabric for background

+ ½ yard (45.72cm) each of assorted white, pink, gray and black prints for strings

+ (30) 5½" (13.97cm) paper foundations, 5 for each block

+ ⅜ yards (34.29cm) solid black fabric for first border

+ ¼ yard (22.86cm) light pink print fabric for second border

+ ½ yard (45.72cm) dark gray print for third border

+ 2¾ yards (251.46cm) backing fabric

+ ⅜ yard (34.29cm) binding fabric

WOF = width of fabric

CUTTING INSTRUCTIONS

From the light gray background fabric, cut:
  (24) 5½" (13.97cm) background squares
  (6) 7" (17.78cm) squares. Sub-cut *each* square corner to corner, twice, to make 4 quarter-square triangles

From the assorted prints in *each* color, cut:
  1" to 2¼" (2.54 to 5.72cm) strings in varying lengths, cutting more 1¼" to 1¾" (3.175 to 4.45cm) strings than others
  Keep each color together.

From the border fabrics, cut:
  (5) 2" (5.08cm) x WOF black strips for the first border
  (5) 1½" (3.81cm) x WOF, light pink print strips for the second border
  (5) 3" (7.62cm) x WOF, dark gray print strips for the third border

From backing fabric, cut:
  (2) 48" (121.92cm) x WOF pieces

From binding fabric, cut:
  (5) 2½" (6.35cm) x WOF strips

CONSTRUCTION OF THE BLOCKS

Each of the six quilt blocks in the Card Trick Quilt is made up of nine different squares. I found it easiest to make six of the same squares at one time.

1. Make six of each of the following colorways using light gray background fabric squares. Refer to Single Half-Square Triangles, page 26.

Make (6) of each

2. Make the side block sections using 5½" (13.97cm) square paper foundations, paying careful attention to the placement of the colors. Refer to Combining to Half and Quarter-Square Triangles, page 20.

Make (6) of each

3. Make six, pink/gray half-square triangle sections and six, white/black half-square triangle sections, using 5½" (13.97 cm) paper foundations. Pay close attention to the color placement and string direction for these sections.

Make (6)

4. Lay out the sections for each block, as shown. Sew the sections into rows and sew the rows together to make six Card Trick blocks.

Make 6

TABLE TOPPER ASSEMBLY

1. Sew the 6 blocks together as shown.

2. For the black border sew the 2" (5.08cm) border strips together into one long strip. Measure the quilt center from side to side. Cut the top and bottom border strips to this size and sew in place.

3. Measure the quilt center from top to bottom. Cut the side border strips to size and sew in place.

4. For the second border sew the 1½" (3.81cm) border strips together into one long strip. Repeat steps 1-2 to add the second border.

5. For the third border sew the 3" (7.62cm) border strips together into one long strip. Repeat steps 1-2 to add the second border.

FINISHING THE TABLE TOPPER

1. Trim the selvages from the (3) 48" (121.92cm) x WOF pieces and sew the pieces together with a generous ¼" (0.64cm) seam. Open the seam and press.

2. Layer the backing, batting, and quilt top together and baste. Quilt as desired.

3. Sew the binding strips together using diagonal seams to create one continuous strip. Press the strip in half lengthwise, wrong sides together, and sew to the raw edge of the quilt top. Fold binding over raw edges and hand stitch in place.

4. For the third border sew the 3" (7.62cm) border strips together into one long strip. Measure from side to side, cut top and bottom border strips to size and sew in place. Measure from top to bottom, cut side border strips to size and sew in place.

Dresden Plate Wall Hanging

Take a simple Dresden Plate to the next level using strings
to make the wedges. This project is relatively straightforward,
but looks complicated and is likely to impress.

FINISHED WALL HANGING SIZE APPROXIMATELY: 20" (50.80cm) SQUARE
FINISHED BLOCK SIZE: 10" (25.40cm) SQUARE

MATERIALS

+ ⅜ yard (34.29cm) for background fabric

+ (6) assorted fat quarters or leftover strips of fabric

+ 6" (15.24cm) square for circle center

+ 7" (17.78cm) square lightweight fusible interfacing

+ ¼ yard (22.86cm) backing fabric

+ ¼ yard (22.86cm) binding fabric

WOF = width of fabric

TOOLS

15° wedge ruler is 9" (22.80cm) long

CUTTING INSTRUCTIONS

From the background print fabric, cut:
(1) 10½" (26.67cm) x WOF strip. From this strip, cut:
(4) 10½" (26.67cm) squares

From *each* of the 6 fat quarters, cut:
A range of 1" to 1¾" (2.54 to 4.45cm) X 22" strings.
Cut the strings in half.

From the binding fabric, cut:
(3) 2½" (6.35cm) x WOF strips

It is OK if some of the
strings are a little crooked.
The unevenness of the
strings adds to the charm
of the design.

CONSTRUCTING THE BLOCKS

1. Refer to Making Dresden Plate Sections, page 44. Sew together four to six of the 10" to 11" (25.40 to 27.94cm) strings, mixing fabrics and width of strings. Press the seam open after adding each string. Add more strings until each string set is at least 7" (17.78cm) wide Make six string sets. Trim each string set to 7" (17.78cm) wide.

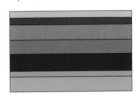

2. Carefully stack and cut three string sets at a time. Cut into wedges using a 15° wedge ruler or template. If using a 15° wedge ruler, place the wedge ruler so that the stack is between the 2" (5.08cm) and 9" (22.86cm) lines on the ruler. (You can mark the line lines on the ruler with tape). Cut (24) wedge sections, you can get four wedges from each string set.

Wedge ruler at 2" (5.08cm) and 9" (22.86cm)

 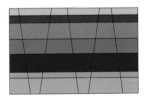

3. Fold the wide (top) section of the wedge in half with right sides together and sew across the top ¼" (0.64cm) from the top edge. Turn the top right side out carefully making the points and press.

¼" (0.64cm)

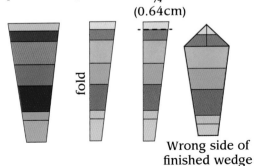

fold

Wrong side of finished wedge

4. Lay out sets of six wedges, mixing the wedges from different string sets. Sew the wedges with the right sides together, using a ¼" (0.64cm) seam. Press the seams open after adding each new wedge. Make four wedge sets.

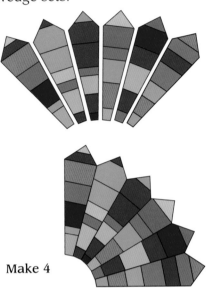

Make 4

5. Pin a wedge set to a 10½" (26.67cm) background square as shown. Baste using a longer stitch in the locations shown to hold it in place for appliqué.

Using a blanket stitch of blind hem stitch, sew along the top edge around each point to appliqué the wedge set into place on the background square. On the back side, trim away excess background fabric between the two basting lines.

6. Sew the four blocks together as shown.

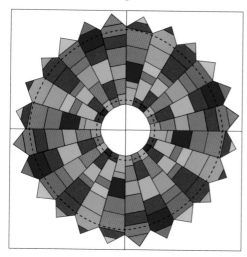

7. Cut a 5½" (13.97cm) circle using the circle template on page 103. Place the 7" (17.78cm) square of lightweight fusible interfacing with the fusible side (the slightly pebbly side) facing up. Place the right side of the circle face down on top of the interfacing.

8. Sew in place by sewing ¼" (0.64cm) from the edge of the circle. Trim with scissors to the edge of the fabric circle.

9. Make a slit in the interfacing. Carefully turn the circle right side out and finger press around the edges to make a smooth circle. Pin into place on the center of the wedge circle. Press. The fusible interfacing will hold the circle in place during appliqué. Appliqué using a blanket stitch or blind hem stitch.

10. Remove the basting stitches from the wedge sections. Remove excess fabric from behind the appliqué.

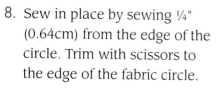

FINISHING THE WALL HANGING

1. Cut a piece of batting and backing fabric several inches larger than the finished size of the Dresden Plate block.

2. Layer the backing, batting, and quilt block together and baste. Quilt as desired.

3. Sew the binding strips together using diagonal seams to create one continuous strip. Press the strip in half lengthwise, wrong sides together, and sew to the raw edge of the block. Fold binding over raw edges and hand stitch in place. Add a hanging sleeve if desired.

7" (17.78cm)
WEDGE TEMPLATE

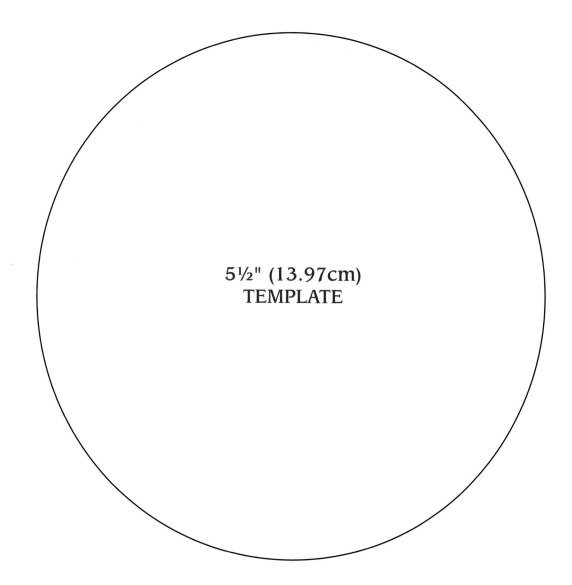

5½" (13.97cm)
TEMPLATE

Dresden Plate Table Runner

Six wedge sections are applied to each of eight squares, then quarter square setting triangles are added to make this stunning runner.
For a table or bed, this runner is eye-catching!

It works for a table or bed runner.
Either way, the movement created by the curvy blocks will be eye-catching!

FINISHED TABLE RUNNER SIZE APPROXIMATELY:
22" X 62" (55.88 X 157.48CM)
FINISHED BLOCK SIZE: 9½" SQUARE

MATERIALS

◆ 1½ yards (137.16cm) white fabric for background

◆ (6) assorted fat quarters or the equivalent in leftover fabrics.

◆ 1¾ yard (160.02cm) for backing fabric

◆ ⅜ yard (34.29cm) for binding fabric

WOF = width of fabric

CUTTING INSTRUCTIONS

From the white background fabric, cut:

(2) 10½" (26.67cm) x WOF strips. From the strips, cut:
(8) 10½" squares

(2) 15½" (39.37cm) x WOF strips. From the strips, cut:
(3) 15½" (39.37cm) squares. Sub-cut the squares, twice, diagonally, to make quarter-square triangles. (Only 10 will be used)

(1) 8" (20.32cm) square. Sub-cut the square, diagonally to make two half-square triangles.

From the binding fabric, cut:
(5) 2½" (6.35cm) x WOF strips

From the backing fabric, cut:
(2) 30" (76.20cm) x WOF pieces

CONSTRUCTING THE BLOCKS

1. Refer to Making Dresden Plate Sections, page 44. Sew together four to six assorted fat quarter strings, mixing fabrics and width of strings. Press the seam open after adding each string. Add more strings until each string set is at least 7" (17.78cm) wide Make six string sets. Trim each string set to 7" (17.78cm) wide.

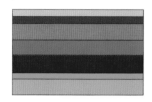

2. Carefully stack and cut three string sets at a time. Cut into wedges using a 15° wedge ruler or template. If using a 15° wedge ruler, place the wedge ruler so that the stack is between the 2" (5.08cm) and 9" (22.86cm) lines on the ruler. Cut (24) wedge sections, you can get four wedges from each string set.

Wedge ruler at 2" (5.08cm) and 9" (22.86cm)

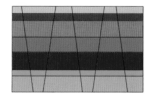

3. Fold the wide (top) section of a wedge in half with right sides together and sew across the top ¼" (0.64cm) from the top edge. Turn the top right side out, carefully making the points and press.

¼" (0.64cm)

fold

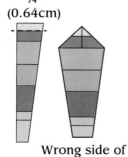

Wrong side of finished wedge

4. Lay out six wedges, mixing them from different string sets. Sew the wedges with the right sides together, using a ¼" (0.64cm) seam. Press the seams open after adding each new wedge Make four wedge sets.

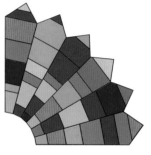

5. Pin a wedge set to a 10½" (26.67cm) background square. Baste, using a longer stitch in the locations shown to hold it in place for appliqué.

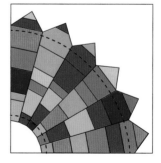

Using a blanket stitch or blind hem stitch, sew along the top edge around each point to appliqué the wedge set into place on the background square. On the back side, trim away excess background fabric between the two basting lines.

TABLE RUNNER ASSEMBLY

1. Lay out all the runner pieces as shown in diagram.

2. Sew together in diagonal columns. Press seams open.

3. Sew the diagonal columns together. Press seams open.

FINISHING THE TABLE RUNNER

1. Trim the selvages and sew the (2) 30" (76.20cm) x WOF backing pieces together to make a 30" x 80" (76.20 x 203.20cm) backing. Press the seam.

2. Layer the backing, batting, and runner top together and baste. Quilt as desired.

3. Sew the binding strips together using diagonal seams to create one continuous strip. Press the strip in half lengthwise, wrong sides together, and sew to the raw edge of the block. Fold binding over raw edges and hand stitch in place.

Any number of appliqué stitches can be used to attach the dresden plate wedges, but my favorite is a blanket stitch. If your machine has stitch options, attaching them will go quickly. For a change of pace, hand stitch them. It can be quite calming!

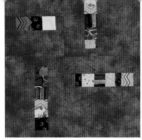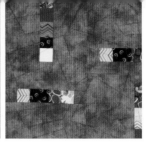

This Way and That Quilt

This quilt uses a simple concept. String sets are pieced and cut into sections and placed vertically into square blocks. By varying the placement of the string sections with in a solid color block, and turning the block vertically or horizontally, the eye moves from one area of the quilt to the next. Adding a string pieced border echoes the strings used in the quilt center.

FINISHED QUILT SIZE APPROXIMATELY: 74" X 93" (187.96 X 236.22cm)
FINISHED BLOCK SIZE: 9½" (24.13cm) SQUARE

MATERIALS

✦ 4½ yards (411.48cm) rust blender fabric for background

✦ (10) assorted fat quarters or equivalent fabric scraps for pieced string sets and borders

✦ 5¾ yard (525.78cm) backing fabric

✦ ¾ yard (68.58cm) binding fabric

WOF = width of fabric

CUTTING INSTRUCTIONS

From the rust blender background fabric, cut:

(16) 9" (22.86cm) x WOF strips. From *each* strip, cut: (4) 10" x 9" (25.40 x 22.86cm) rectangles for a total of (63) background rectangles
Note: These pieces are not square as you might expect since the string inserts will add to the size.

(7) 2" (5.08cm) x WOF strips. Cut *each* strip in half.

From the assorted fat quarters, cut:
21" (53.34cm) long strips varying from 1½" to 2¼" (3.81 to 5.72cm)

From the backing fabric, cut:
(2) 103" (261.62cm) x WOF strips

From the binding fabric, cut:
(10) 2½" (6.35cm) x WOF strips

> This is an easy quilt. Changing the background or strings can provide a very different look.

Quilting by Yessant Habetz

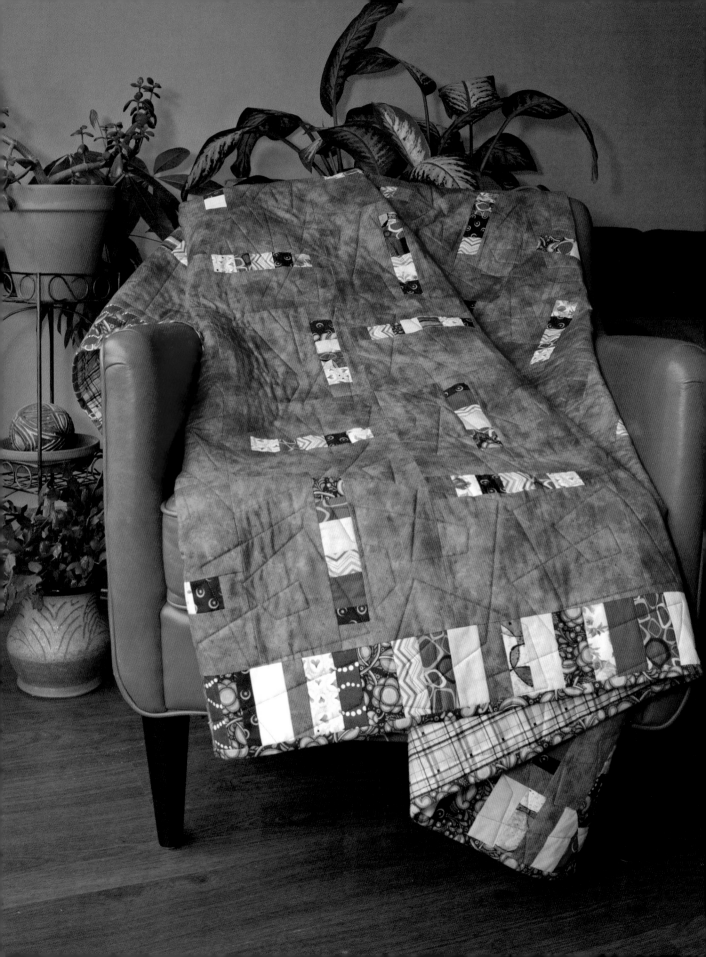

BLOCK CONSTRUCTION

1. Using the 1½" to 2¼" (3.81 to 5.72cm) strips of fabric for string inserts and border: Sew four to five 21" (53.34cm) strings together lengthwise, mixing values, print types and string widths. The strip set should be at least 7" (17.78cm) wide.

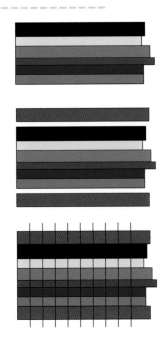

2. Add a 2" X 21" (5.08 x 53.34cm) strip of red background fabric to the top and bottom of each string set. Make (7) string sets for string inserts. Set aside the rest of this fabric for borders.

3. Cut (9) 2" (5.08cm) strips from each string set to make a total of (63) 2" (5.08cm) pieced strings.

4. Cut a 10" x 9" (25.40 x 22.86cm) rectangle vertically into two rectangles. Using ¼" (0.64cm) seams, sew one side of a 2" (5.08cm) string set to the left rectangle; then sew to the right rectangle. Trim the ends of the 2" (5.08cm) string set even with the block. The block should now be 10" (25.40cm) square.

5. Make a total of 63 blocks, varying the location where you cut the 10" x 9" (25.40 x 22.86cm)rectangle.

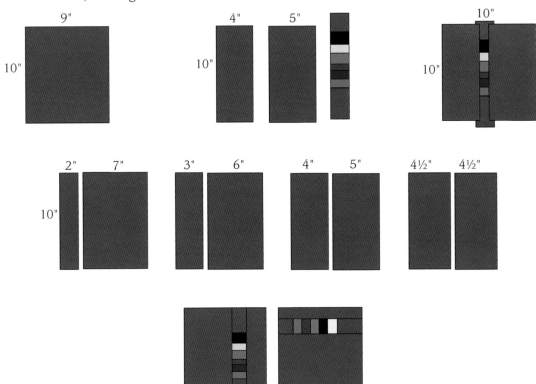

CONSTRUCTING THE BORDER

1. Using the rest of the 1½" to 2¼" (3.81 to 5.72cm) strips, make strip sets for the border by sewing together (10) of the 21" (53.34cm) strings of fabric. Mix values, print types and string widths.

2. From each string set, cut (4) 4" (10.16cm) strips.

3. Sew the 4" (10.16cm) strips of string sets together end to end into long border sections, mixing string sections.

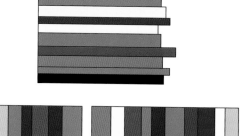

CONSTRUCTING THE QUILT

1. Lay out the quilt blocks in nine rows of seven blocks. Sew the blocks together to make the rows. Sew the rows together to complete the quilt center.

2. Measure the quilt from side to side and add another 10" (25.40cm) to allow for mitering the corners. Cut the top and bottom border sections to this size.

3. Mark the centers of the top and bottom of the quilt and the center of the borders. Align the centers and sew the top and bottom borders in place. Stop sewing ¼" (0.64cm) from the corners.

4. Measure the length of the quilt, including the borders, add another 10" (25.40cm) and cut (2) side border sections to this size.

5. Mark the center of the sides of the quilt and the center of the side borders. Align the centers and sew the side borders in place. Stop sewing ¼" (0.64cm) from the corners.

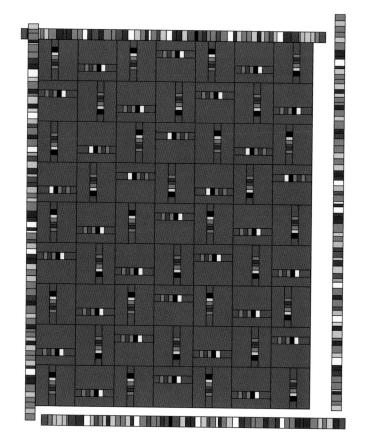

6. Lay the quilt corner right side up on an ironing board. Extend the borders so the vertical border strip overlays the horizontal one.

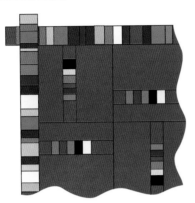

7. Fold the vertical border strip at a 45° angle and press.

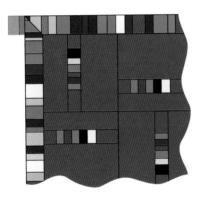

8. Fold the quilt top, right sides together, on the diagonal so the edges of the two border strips align. Pin the borders together along the creased line.

9. Sew on the creased line to make the mitered seam.

10. Trim the seam to ¼" (0.64cm) and press open.

11. Repeat on the remaining corners.

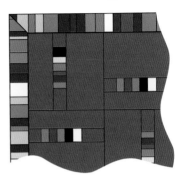

FINISHING THE QUILT

1. Trim the selvages from the (2) 103" (261.62cm) x WOF strips. Sew with a generous ¼" (0.64cm) seam. Press the seam open.

2. Layer the backing, batting, and quilt top together and baste. Quilt as desired.

3. Sew the binding strips together on the diagonal to make one long strip. Press the strip wrong sides together. Sew the strip to the quilt top, matching the raw edges with the edge of the quilt. Fold the binding to the back, covering raw edges and hand stitch in place.

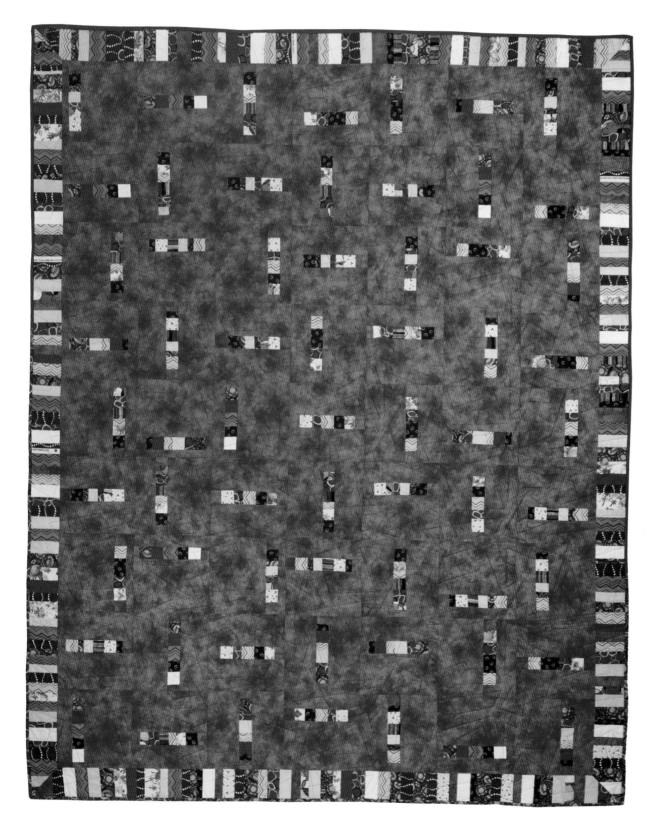

Confetti Columns Quilt

Using fat quarters in two colors, bright pink and black, strips are sewn together to make strip sets. After cutting the strip sets apart, mixing, and sewing them together, you create columns of small pieces. Add bits of pink to the black strip sets for a bit more contrast.

FINISHED QUILT SIZE APPROXIMATELY: 88" X 90" (223.52 X 228.60cm)
FINISHED COLUMN SIZE: 22" X 90" (55.88 X 228.60cm)

MATERIALS

✦ 3½ yards (320.04cm) white fabric for background

✦ 10 assorted black fat quarters

✦ 10 assorted pink fat quarters

✦ 7⅔ yard (700.43cm) for 42" (106.68cm) wide fabric
3 yard (274.32cm) for 108" (274.32cm) wide fabric

✦ ¾ yard (68.58cm)for binding fabric

WOF = width of fabric

CUTTING INSTRUCTIONS

From *each* black and pink fat quarter, keeping the colors separate, cut:

(1) 3½" x 21" (8.89 x 53.34cm) strip
(1) 3" x 21" (8.89 x 53.34cm) strip
(1) 2½" x 21" (6.35 x 53.34cm) strip
(2) 2" x 21" (6.35 x 53.34cm) strips
(1) 1¾" x 21" (4.45 x 53.34cm) strip
(1) 1½" x 21" (3.81 x 53.34cm) strip

Set aside any extra fabric.

From the backing fabric, cut:

(3) 100" (254.00cm) x WOF strips
OR
(1) 100" (254.00cm) x WOF piece

From the binding fabric, cut:

(10) 2½" (6.35cm) x WOF strips

The pink and black prints against the white background create a very dramatic quilt.

Quilting by Joyce Brenner

Work with one color at a time to make the confetti column segments. You can add interest by adding an occasional strip of pink fabric to the black strip set or vice versa. Or, add a random, narrow 1½" (3.81cm) background strip to a strip set. Refer to the quilt photo for inspiration.

COLUMN ASSEMBLY

1. Make pink assorted and black assorted 21" (53.34cm) strip sets, by sewing 4 to 6 strips together. Mix fabrics and widths within each strip set. The objective is to have varying strip widths within a set. Press seams to one side.

2. Measure each strip set. Add enough background fabric to make 12½" x 21" (31.75 x 53.34cm) sets. For instance, if the strip set is 6" (15.24cm), add a 7" (17.78cm) strip of background fabric. If the strip set is 9" (22.86cm), add a 4" (10.16cm) strip of background fabric. Press seams open.

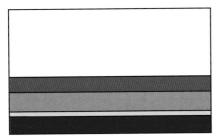 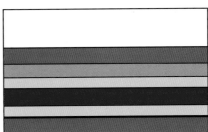

3. From each 12½" x 21" (31.75 x 53.34cm) pink and black strip sets, cut the following segments:

(1) 3½" (8.89cm) segment

(1) 3" (7.62cm) segment

(2) 2½" (6.35cm) segments

(1) 2" (5.08cm) segment

(2) 1½" (3.81cm) segments

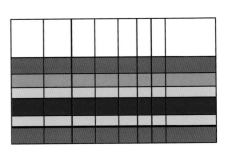

From what is left in each strip set, cut segments of any size.

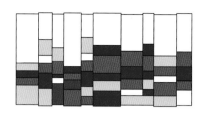

4. Sew together, 8 to 10 strip segments from step 3, side to side, varying the strips to create an uneven grouping, as shown. Continue making pink strip segments and black strip segments in this way until most of the strip segments have been used up. Press seams open to reduce bulk and keep seams flat.

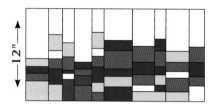

5. Because the row of segments gets a little crooked when sewn together, trim each column section to 12" (30.48cm).

6. Sew segment sections together to make four, long column sections of each color, each about 88" (223.52cm).Press seams open.

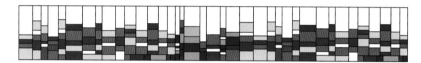

7. Sew two pink column sections together, joining the pink sides. Sew with a generous ¼" (0.64cm) seam. Press seam open. Repeat with the other set of pink column sections to make two pink columns.

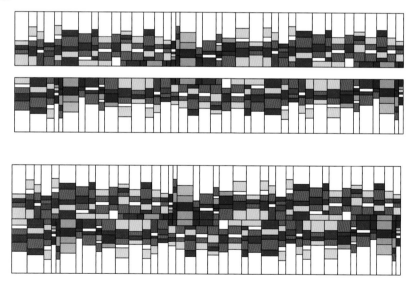

8. Repeat step 7 with the black column sections. Make two black columns.

QUILT ASSEMBLY

Sew the columns together in order from left to right. Press seams open. Trim as needed to straighten sides and corners.

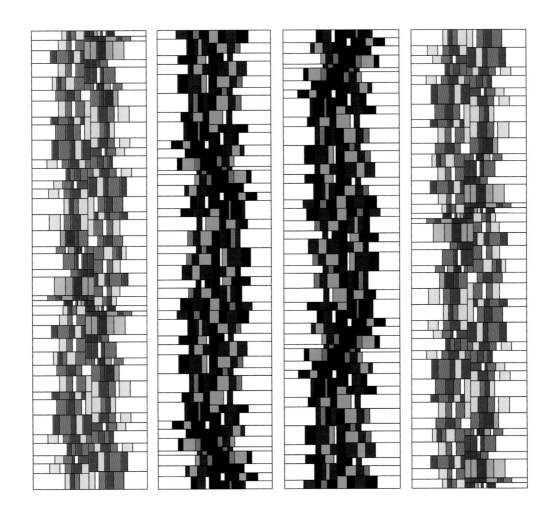

FINISHING THE QUILT

1. Trim the selvages from (3) 100" (254.00cm) x WOF strips or (1) 100" (254.00cm) x WOF piece. Sew together with a generous ¼" (0.64cm) seam. Press seam open.

2. Layer the backing, batting, and quilt top together and baste. Quilt as desired.

3. Sew the binding strips together on the diagonal to make one long strip. Press the strip wrong sides together. Sew the strip to the quilt top, matching the raw edges with the edge of the quilt. Fold the binding to the back, covering raw edges and hand stitch in place.

Four Seasons of Trees Wall Hangings

Some years ago, I completed an embroidery kit with four trees, showing the same tree during the four seasons. I was so inspired by that kit, I made a wall hanging with trees using strings.

FINISHED WALL HANGING SIZE APPROXIMATELY:16½" X 18½" (42 X 47cm)

MATERIALS

+ 1 yard (228.6cm) blue fabric for background

+ 1 yard (228.6cm) of dark print for tree trunk and branches

+ ½ to ¾ yards (57.15 to 68.58cm) of seasonal fabric for *each* tree. Try a mix of 5-6 fabric colors.

+ 1⅜ yards (125.73cm) backing fabric

+ ¼ yard (22.86cm) of seasonal binding fabric for *each* tree

+ (8) 9" x 18" (22.86 x 45.72cm) paper foundations

WOF = width of fabric

CUTTING INSTRUCTIONS

From the blue background fabric, cut:

(8) 2½" (6.35cm) x WOF strips. From the strips, cut:
(2) 2½" x 8" (6.35 x 20.32cm) strips for borders

(1) 4" (10.16cm) x WOF strip. From the strip, cut:
(8) 4" (10.16cm) squares for bottom corners

(1) 7" (17.78cm) x WOF strip. From the strip, cut:
(4) 9" x 7" (22.86 x 17.78cm) rectangles for bottom corners

1½" (3.81cm) x WOF to 2½" (6.35cm) x WOF for bottom corners

From the dark print fabric, cut:

(2) 2½" (6.35cm) x WOF pieces
From the pieces, cut:
(2) 2½" x 18" (6.35 x 45.72cm) pieces for tree trunks

(4) 2½" (6.35cm) squares for the tree trunk bottom borders.

Cut a few 1½" to 2½" (3.81 to 6.35cm) x WOF strips for tree branches. Cut more strings as needed.

From *each* of the seasonal fabrics, cut:
a few 1" to 1¾" (2.54 to 4.45cm) strips. Cut the strips as long as your fabric pieces allow. Cut about half of each fabric piece. Cut more strings as needed.

From the backing fabric, cut:
(2) 24" (60.96cm) x WOF pieces.
From the pieces, cut:
(2) 20" x 24" (50.80 x 60.96cm) rectangles.

From the binding fabric, cut:
(3) 2½" (6.35cm) x WOF strips for *each* wall hanging.

PREPARE THE PAPER FOUNDATIONS

1. Cut (2) 9" x 18" (22.86 x 45.72cm) paper foundations. One will be used to piece the left side of the tree and the other for the right side of the tree.

2. Use pencil to mark the angle for placing the strings. For the left side of the tree, place a ruler at the top left corner to 1½" (3.81cm) above the lower right corner. Make the corresponding line on the foundation for the right side of the tree.

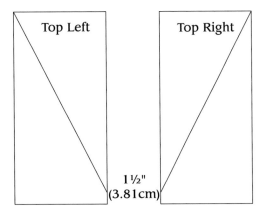

3. Identify the top left and top right sections of the tree, as shown.

CONSTRUCTION OF THE TREE PANELS

1. Refer to Making Tree Panels, page 40, to make the right and left tree sections.

Note: Work on one tree at a time. Work on the right and left side of the tree separately. Reduce the stitch length a little from what you usually use to make it easier to remove the paper foundation.

2. Trim both sides of the tree to 8" x 18" (20.32 x 45.72cm). Carefully remove paper.

3. From the 2½" x 18" (6.35 x 45.72cm) tree trunk fabric, trim the piece as shown.

4. Sew the tree trunk to the left tree section with the narrow end at the top of the tree. Press the seam towards the tree trunk.

5. Sew the right tree section to the trunk. Press the seam towards the tree trunk.

6. Trim the tree to 15" x 17" (38.10 x 43.18cm).

7. Draw a line from corner to corner on two, 4" (10.16cm) blue background squares.

8. Place a square, right side down, on one corner of the tree. Sew along the drawn line. Trim the corner ¼" (0.64cm) from the seam line. Open and press the corner. Repeat for the other corner.

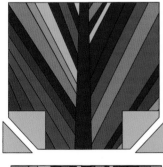

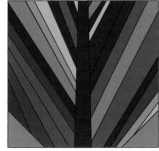

9. Mark the top center of the tree panel. Make a mark from each top corner, 6" (15.24cm) down each side of the panel. Place a ruler along the marks to cut off each corner of the tree panel.

10. Using the (4) 9" x 7" (22.86 x 17.78cm) background rectangles, stack two sets of (2) rectangles right side up. Cut in half diagonally as shown to make (4) left and (4) right top corners.

11. Align the right background fabric wedge, from step 10, along the right corner of the tree panel. Sew in place and press the seam away from the tree. Repeat for the left corner.

12. Trim tree to 15" x 17" (38.10 x 43.18cm).

ADDING THE BORDERS

1. Using a ¼" (0.64cm) seam allowance, sew (1) 2½" (6.35cm) square of dark print the ends of (2) 2½" x 8" (6.35 x 20.32cm) strips of background fabric. Press the seams open.

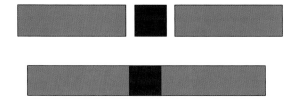

2. Sew this strip to the bottom of the tree with a ¼" (0.64cm) seam, carefully matching the tree trunk seams. Press away from the tree. Trim the right and left edges as needed.

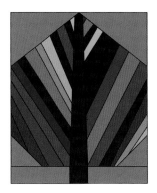

3. Sew a 2½" x 15" (6.35 x 38.10cm) background strip to the top of the tree and press away from the tree.

4. Sew one 2½" x 17.5" (6.35 x 44.45cm) to each side of the tree section, using ¼" (0.64cm) seam. Press away from the tree.

FINISHING THE WALLHANGINGS

1. Layer the backing, batting, and tree panel together and baste. Quilt as desired.

2. Trim the borders to 2" (5.08cm) from the seam line to straighten the edges of the tree panel.

3. Sew the binding strips together on the diagonal to make one long strip. Press the strip wrong sides together. Sew the strip to the tree panel, matching the raw edges with the edge of the quilt. Fold the binding to the back, covering raw edges and hand stitch in place.

I have always lived in the Midwest, so the trees and
color used reflect my experience with the seasonal changes.

In the spring, greens are lighter and vary quite a bit
in color.

Summer trees tend to be more uniform in color
and the greens are darker than the spring.

During fall, trees start turning red, brown, gold,
and rust, depending on the tree.

In winter, more branches can be seen because
there are few, if any, leaves left.

Terms and Definitions

Background Fabric: foundations that are left in place after strings are sewn to them

Binding: provides a line around the edge of a quilt

Borders: used to frame the quilt design and give it a finished look

Crooked strings: strings that are sewn on other strings at an angle

Diagonal square: created when strings are sewn diagonally to a foundation square

Disappearing strings: strings that don't make it all the way from one end of the block to the other

Focal point: center of interest or where viewer's eye is drawn

Geometric: stripes, dots, chevrons, circles, plaid fabrics

Hue: shade or name of the color such as blue, green, gray, purple, etc.

Intensity: the strength or vividness of a color

Line: created by sashing or strings between or within blocks

Monochromatic: having one color or shades of one color

Novelty: representational fabrics ranging from cartoon-like and playful to very realistic

Proportion: balance of sashing, border and block size in relation to the whole quilt and its other parts

Removable foundations: paper or paper-type products to which strings are sewn; foundation is removed after strings are trimmed

Representational: fabric that is meant to look like or resemble something that exists in the physical world; for example, cars, pigs, trees, leaves, buttons, flowers

Rough-cut foundations: removable or permanent foundations that are oversized; they are cut to size after strings have been added

Sashing: separates blocks or rows of blocks to add a line element

Shape: squares, triangles, circles that make up block designs

Solids: fabrics that are one color

Strings: strips of fabric of varying widths and shapes

Value: lightness or darkness of the color; the lightest color value is white and the darkest is black

Variation: changing lines, shapes and other elements so they are not repetitive in the design

About the Author

Mary Hogan, a self-taught sewer, began her sewing career making clothes for dolls. In her teens, she moved into making garments, stuffed toys and dolls. After dabbling in numerous crafts, she found quilting in the 1990's. Now retired from her day job, Mary devotes nearly all her time to quilting, designing, and teaching.

She uses as many fabrics as possible in each quilt and likes improvisation, rarely knowing how a quilt will turn out when she begins. Mary has made hundreds of quilts.

Passionate about sharing quilting with others, she teaches regularly at The Quilting Season in Saline, Michigan. She believes that classes should provide opportunities to learn, to practice new skills, and, above all, classes should be fun. This is Mary's third quilting book.

Mary has a BS in Nursing from Loyola University in Chicago, an MS in Public Health Nursing from the University of Illinois at Chicago, and a PhD in Health Services from the University of Michigan and has held a variety of positions related to nursing and health care. She lives in Michigan with her husband, six sewing machines, and a growing stash of quilts, fabric, thread, and yarn.

Resources

Moda: Valley by Sherri and Chelsi

Moda: Black Tie Affair by BasicGrey

Houts, J & Wright, J. A. 2009. Circle of Nine: 24 Stunning and Creative Quilts: One Unique Quilt Setting, Urbandale IA: Landauer. Circling Geese